**NATIONAL
PLANNING
ASSOCIATION**

Canadian
Industrial
Policy

**PETER MORICI
ARTHUR J.R. SMITH
SPERRY LEA**

CANADIAN INDUSTRIAL POLICY

NPA Report No. 193
June 1982
Price $10.00

ISBN 0-89068-063-9
Library of Congress Catalog Card Number 82-81566

Short quotations with appropriate credit permissible.

NATIONAL PLANNING ASSOCIATION
A voluntary association incorporated under the laws of
the District of Columbia
1606 New Hampshire Avenue, N.W.
Washington, D.C. 20009

Contents

Canadian Industrial Policy

by Peter Morici,
Arthur J.R. Smith and
Sperry Lea

TABLES AND FIGURES

Forward

For over a quarter century, the National Planning Association has been addressing the major issues surrounding Canadian-American relations. Since 1957, it has served as the U.S. cosponsor of the Canadian-American Committee, a group of private-sector leaders in both countries which has published 49 studies and policy statements mostly on bilateral economic issues. More recently, NPA has cosponsored a series of nine studies in the "Canada-U.S. Prospects" series.[1] Through these activities, members of NPA's staff have become intimately acquainted with the development of Canadian policies regarding bilateral trade, foreign ownership and numerous other themes which Ottawa is currently gathering into a serious attempt to form a national industrial policy.

As they have become aware of various unilateral Canadian initiatives that are major elements in this effort, many Americans have shown growing concern over their implications for American business and labor. Meanwhile, some have come to feel that the time was propitious to expand mutually beneficial ties with our North American neighbors. Reflecting both these views, the U.S. Congress in 1979 directed the executive branch to review the potential for expanded U.S. economic relations with other North American countries. As part of its response to this mandate, the Administration turned to NPA in that year for a review of the major bilateral and multilateral issues confronting the two countries, and in 1980 it asked NPA to undertake a broad study of Canadian industrial policy.[2] The following report is based on that work funded principally by the U.S. Department of Commerce, updated to reflect the considerable subsequent developments.

NPA was fortunate to have on the staff at that time three persons with 50 years combined experience in the United States and Canada working on bilateral economic issues.

Peter Morici, the study's principal author, is the Associate Director of NPA's International Division and is currently serving as the U.S. Research Director of the Canadian-American Committee. He is the author of *Canada-United States Trade and Economic Interdependence* and holds a Ph.D. in Economics.

Arthur J.R. Smith, a Canadian, was at the time President of NPA and is now associated with Woods Gordon. His previous positions include President of the Conference Board in Canada and Chairman of the Economic Council of Canada. Mr. Smith served as the founding director of the Private Planning Association of Canada, later to become the C.D. Howe Institute. He holds a Ph.D. in Economics. In preparing this study, he was mainly responsible for much of the historical material in Chapters 1 and 2.

---

1   In both cases, the Canadian cosponsor has been the C.D. Howe Institute in Montreal.

2   *Perspectives on Commercial Policy: The United States and Canada in the Eighties* and *Canadian Industrial Policy*, prepared for the U.S. Department of Commerce under contract no. TA-79-SAC-01867.

Sperry Lea, a Vice President of NPA, has served the Canadian-American Committee for over 17 years, mostly as its U.S. Research Director and now as its U.S. Secretary. He was responsible for the section on Canadian foreign investment policy and the appendix material on the automotive industry.

The authors completed their research in 1981 and the work was current to the end of that year, although some additional updating was undertaken. This study represents the findings and views of the authors, which are not necessarily those of NPA or its trustees, the Canadian-American Committee or its members, or the Department of Commerce.

I am pleased to make available to the public this document, which, dealing as it does with the source of considerable strains between the largest trade and investment partnership in the world, can provide a factual basis for a better understanding of some important developments in Canadian-American relations, and ones that are relevant to the wider world as well.

June 1982

Alexander C. Tomlinson
President, NPA

Introduction

Many industrial nations, in particular France and Japan, have attempted to develop and integrate government policies and programs into consistent industrial policies. Their goals have been to improve the relative competitive position and performance of selected sectors of their economies, fostering growth in new industries and easing adjustment in mature and declining activities. In contrast, the United States, with its commitment to the market process, has never developed any such *explicit* industrial policy, although it uses some of the same policy instruments—e.g., subsidies, low interest loans and tax concessions. Historically, Canada's approach has fluctuated between the examples set by France and Japan, on the one hand, and the United States, on the other.

Canada shares the U.S. commitment to the enterprise system and belief in the effectiveness of the market process. Although it is difficult to generalize about a country whose population is so geographically dispersed and culturally diverse, it seems fair to say that most Canadians have not yet embraced the European concepts of Social Democracy or Indicative Planning. The economic philosophies and policies of the two major national political parties attest to this. However, faced with the problems of an economy one-tenth the size of the United States, of a geographically scattered population, of powerful economic and financial relationships with U.S. markets, and of maintaining a national identity, Canada has experimented with various concepts of industrial policy over the past 100 years. And Canadian governments have intervened more in the market process to achieve industrial development goals than their U.S. counterparts.

During the past century, Canada has pursued a variety of programs designed to increase industrial activity and reduce its relative dependence on natural resource exports. For much of Canada's history, the center of these policies has been tariffs. But more recently, with the gradual reduction of tariffs through the multilateral trade negotiations (MTN), attention has increasingly turned to other measures, including industrial incentives and policies to influence the actions of foreign multinational corporations (MNCs) operating in Canada.

Today, many Canadians perceive a need to redirect and better coordinate industrial development efforts, and both within and outside the government there are numerous industrial policy prescriptions. For instance, the Departments of Regional Industrial Expansion and Finance and the influential Cabinet Committee on Economic and Regional Development are actively reevaluating Canada's policies and programs. Many of the provinces are also pursuing ambitious economic development programs, and these have raised concerns in Ottawa about the future of federal leadership in economic policymaking.[1]

---

1 In this study, the terms economic development policies and economic development programs refer to general policies and programs intended to increase the overall level of economic development and activity. The term industrial policy refers to the collection of policies intended to focus the direction and structure of economic development and activity, as well as to increase their levels. Generally, industrial policies are embodied in economic development programs, especially as the latter become more focused and ambitious.

While no explicit statement of Canadian industrial policy has emerged,[2] it is clear that in recent years the federal government has assumed a more activist role not only through greater controls on the activities of foreign investors and the use of industrial incentives, as just noted, but also through the activities of its public corporations, price regulations and incentives in the energy sector and many other industrial policy tools. These initiatives toward a more interventionist Canadian industrial policy have significant consequences for U.S. businesses that sell goods and services or invest in Canada and thus for U.S.-Canadian trade and investment relations. The purpose of this study is to examine the motivations behind, contents of and outlook for Canadian industrial policy and to explore some of its potential consequences for the United States and U.S.-Canadian economic relations.

WHAT IS AN INDUSTRIAL POLICY?

Broadly defined, an industrial policy is the collection of government programs and policies that significantly affect various industries' relative domestic and international competitive position and overall performance. However, this definition, by including virtually all government activities, is too expansive to be useful. A more narrow definition of industrial policy includes only those programs and policies that directly impact on the domestic and/or international competitiveness of individual firms and industries, the employment opportunities and incomes of segments of the labor force, and/or the development of selected regions. The means may consist of a variety of policies and programs, but they share a common characteristic. These measures essentially operate through their effects on the prices (including wages and interest rates) that face firms, workers and consumers and thereby affect choices about production and consumption. Simply, industrial policy measures are designed to affect the allocation of labor and capital resources among industries, the relative size of particular industries, and how fast they grow or decline relative to their domestic and international competitors and the rest of the economy.

All governments pursue policies and programs that to some degree benefit particular industries, labor-force groups and regions. By using explicit industrial strategies, some governments attempt to coordinate such programs to achieve specific policy goals, and thus consciously seek to alter the outcome of the market process for certain sectors of the economy. Other governments have no institutional vehicle to coordinate industrial policy. For example, the United States undertakes many programs that assist particular industries, groups and regions and that have the effect of an implicit industrial policy. But U.S. policy lacks a consistent theme, and no institutional vehicle exists for resolving the conflicts that may arise among the goals and means of various programs. Many programs influence the end results of the market process, but no attempt is made to conform an outcome of that process to the achievement of a set of objectives.

Current Canadian industrial policy is also implicit rather than explicit. But unlike U.S. policy, Canadian policy cannot be characterized as rudderless; it has some com-

---

2   On November 12, 1981, the government of Canada released *Economic Development for Canada in the 1980s*. This document, prepared by a special Cabinet committee chaired by Finance Minister Allan J. MacEachen, lays out in general terms the government's economic development objectives. In our view, the objectives are too broad for the statement to be characterized as an explicit industrial strategy or policy.

mon elements and consistency, at least at the aspiration level, in its collection of diverse programs. Further, the so-called Envelope System for policy planning and financial management, particularly that part under the Cabinet Committee on Economic and Regional Development, is a potential institutional vehicle for industrial policy formulation, implementation and coordination.

UNDERLYING THEMES IN CANADIAN INDUSTRIAL POLICY

Since Confederation in 1867, Canadian policymakers have had to deal with the conflicts inherent in Canada's considerable level of economic integration with the United States.

Small in terms of population, Canada has at times found closer commercial integration with the United States attractive because of the efficiency and income benefits that can be achieved through expansion of trade and more open transfers of technical and other expertise. The United States is an even stronger magnet because Canada's population is geographically dispersed and divided between two basic language groups, making the draw of U.S. markets greater in some parts of the country than that of its own commercial centers. This natural attraction, coupled with Canada's cultural diversity and lack of a well-defined national identity, have created what many perceive to be a threat of cultural absorption—and its consequences for political integration. Hence, in this context, commercial integration with the United States, while attractive on economic grounds, carries with it deep fears about the potential loss of Canadian independence. In seeking to understand past Canadian industrial policies and to make judgments about their future course, *it is difficult to overestimate the consequences of this fundamental political and cultural reality.*

Nevertheless, close interrelationships have developed with the United States through trade and the relatively free flow of capital between the two countries. These have evolved not through the establishment of a formal economic community or trade area, but rather through the establishment of U.S. subsidiaries in Canada, and vice versa, and a gradual reduction of trade barriers, primarily concluded through multilateral trade negotiations. As beneficial as the flows of goods, services and capital have been, they have posed problems for Canadian industrial policy, which has its origins in attempts to exploit comparative advantages in natural resources while still developing manufacturing industries.

Historically, Canada has displayed comparative advantages in the resource-based sectors—such as grains, fisheries, forestry products, fossil fuels, and minerals—and in some closely related processing and capital-intense industries—such as nonferrous metals and paper products. At least until recently, unilateral elimination of Canadian trade barriers would probably have led to more specialization in natural resource areas and less domestic activity in processing and other aspects of manufacturing. This would have occurred particularly because the natural forces pushing Canada toward resource production and exports have been enhanced by the tariff structures of Canada's principal industrial trading partners, whose average tariffs have risen with the level of processing.[3] The Tokyo Round tariff reductions being implemented during the 1980–87 period should significantly reduce this problem.

---

3   In contrast, multilateral elimination of Canada's and other countries' trade barriers might not have led to greater specialization in natural resource areas, as Canadian industry's opportunities for efficient production would have been less limited by a small domestic market.

Many Canadians, however, do not perceive specialization in resource extraction and related industries as the most beneficial course for industrial development. They feel these sectors are not capable of providing adequate employment opportunities for the nation's well-educated, highly skilled labor force and have voiced considerable concern, especially during the 1950s and '60s, over the outmigration of highly skilled manpower and university-trained professionals. Such specialization makes Canada particularly vulnerable to fluctuations in resource markets. Consequently, many aspects of Canadian international and domestic economic policies are being designed to encourage further processing of natural resource and manufacturing industries, especially in the R&D-intense, high technology activities seen as potentially able to generate high quality employment opportunities.

In addition, Canada, like the United States, experienced a rising unemployment problem during the 1970s as its labor force grew at an exceptionally rapid pace. Therefore, projects and initiatives that could yield large employment opportunities have been given high priority, and much assistance is provided to relocate the small and scattered labor force from economically depressed areas to those with growing job prospects.

Finally, it is strongly believed that the opportunities and fruits of economic development should be widely and equitably distributed among Canada's regions. Thus, Canada devotes considerable resources to the redistribution of income to lagging regions, to the development of infrastructure there, and to the provision of incentives for industry to locate in high unemployment areas.

APPROACHES TO CANADIAN INDUSTRIAL POLICY

Canadian industry is now faced with the task of restructuring to accommodate the additional international competition that will be created by the Tokyo Round tariff cuts and the continuing export thrust of the newly industrializing countries. While there is some agreement that Canada should increase processing and downstream manufacturing of its natural resources and expand its research-oriented, high technology industries, there are competing prescriptions about how these goals should be achieved. Essentially three types of approaches have emerged.

(1) Freer trade/domestic noninterventionist approach. Proponents of this approach advocate the gradual reduction of trade barriers, coupled with *short-term* safeguards and adjustment assistance for firms and individuals adversely affected by trade. However, in the long run, they do not advocate substantial coordinated government intervention to guide systematically the evolution of the economy's structure. Instead, this group, while acknowledging the need for a limited government role, is inclined to rely on market signals to guide private decisionmakers in identifying and exploiting new opportunities.

(2) Interventionist approach. Proponents believe that Canadian trade barriers must be maintained, at least during a period in which the Canadian economy is restructured, with the assistance of various incentives and other forms of government intervention. They advocate a *substantial* role for the government in guiding the restructuring of the economy and in selecting some of the activities Canadian industry pursues.

(3) Freer trade/domestic interventionist approach. Proponents of this approach advocate the gradual reduction of trade barriers with adjustment assistance to help

import-impacted workers move to new opportunities. However, within this group, there is a strong belief that concerted and coordinated government efforts through various incentives (such as tax breaks, subsidies and preferential loans) and other types of intervention are necessary to ensure that industry exploits new opportunities in world markets created by multilateral tariff reductions. This group has limited faith in what orthodox economists call the adjustment process and is not inclined to rely solely on the market process to guide the evolution of the economy.

Advocates of the second and third approaches face the difficult task of selecting, at least to a limited extent, the sectors to be encouraged and discouraged. The capacity and political will of government policymakers to pick winners and losers are important elements in the debate over the appropriate approach for future Canadian industrial policy.

ORGANIZATION OF THE STUDY

Over the past 30 years, Canada's industrial policies have evolved from a mixture of the first and third approaches to the third approach. Chapter 1 provides a brief historical sketch of developments and issues prior to the 1960s. Chapter 2 continues the story through the 1960s and '70s. Chapter 3 examines the Canadian industrial policy-making apparatus, while Chapter 4 reviews current policy objectives and constraints. Chapter 5 outlines the main elements of Canada's present industrial policy programs, and Chapter 6 reviews some of these important initiatives in three provinces. Chapter 7 examines the main competing views about the appropriate directions for Canadian industrial policy in the 1980s and for its future evolution. It also describes the feasible changes, both political and economic, in Canada's domestic and international industrial policies. Chapter 8 presents a brief assessment of the consequences for the United States and for U.S.-Canadian relations.

Throughout the study, except in Chapter 6, primary emphasis is placed on federal policy. Many of the provinces are pursuing ambitious industrial policies of their own, which have substantial consequences for particular regions of the United States, and these are worthy of a separate, systematic study.

1

Early Developments

Canada's early native patterns of economic evolution were disrupted and radically changed by the intrusions of Europeans who progressively discovered the great natural wealth of what is today the Canadian nation, and who over time began to link manpower, skills, capital, technology, and other productive elements to production and substantial export of these natural resources. The course of this resource development, starting with the rich East Coast fisheries and extending through the fur trade, the lumber industry, agriculture, and minerals, has been well documented in the literature of Canadian economic history.[1] Commerce and basic resource development, and consequent linkages with Europe, were, therefore, the key elements in the overall economic progress of Canada for an extended period essentially beginning in the seventeenth century and continuing for over two centuries.

In the nineteenth century, the industrial revolution that had gathered momentum in Europe could hardly be a geographically contained phenomenon. Elements of it increasingly spread throughout many enterprising societies with cultural roots in Europe. Canada was caught up, at least on the periphery, in this development and sought ways to process further its natural resources and indigenous, although often rather localized, manufacturing activities, such as iron foundries, flour mills, apparel factories, and food processing plants. The (limited) success of these measures was inevitably constrained by lack of access to the larger markets necessary for more specialized and increased scales of production and technological applications.

The limited free trade arrangement with the United States under the Elgin Marcy Treaty of 1854 was a dynamic factor in Canadian development for more than a decade. The treaty covered agricultural and forest products, metals and ores, animals, fish and their products, and a small group of manufactures. In total, about 90 percent of U.S. imports from Canada and approximately 55 percent of Canada's imports from the United States were duty free between 1855 and 1866.[2]

Either party could abrogate the treaty on a one-year notice, an option adopted by the United States in 1865, which terminated the treaty the following year in a sharp setback to Canadian development progress. After Confederation in 1867, the new Dominion of Canada attempted to persuade the United States to renew the treaty or enter into a more extensive arrangement, but without success. In 1879, Canada adopted a second-best development strategy in the National Policy that sought to "build a country" along an east-west axis. Its elements were a high tariff protection policy to encourage domestic manufacturing; a transportation policy, including construction of a transcontinental railroad, to foster east-west connections; and an open

---

1   See especially the brilliant sequence of basic studies by the noted economic historian Harold Innis.

2   Anna Guthrie, "Brief History of Canadian American Reciprocity," in Sperry Lea, *A Canada-U.S. Free Trade Arrangement: Survey of Possible Characteristics* (Washington, D.C.: Canadian-American Committee, 1963), p. 85.

immigration policy to help thicken the thin coast-to-coast demographic ribbon north of the U.S. border.

In the late 1880s and '90s, the United States made several overtures concerning the establishment of a trade area, but Canada was less eager at that time. The two countries were unable to agree on issues such as the nature of the arrangement (the United States favored a customs union as opposed to more limited free trade) and the extension of preferences to other countries (Canada granted such preferences to Great Britain in the late 1890s).

In industrial terms (that is, with special focus on processing and manufacturing activities), the National Policy was not a great success. In the 1880s and through much of the next decade, the country experienced relatively serious depressed conditions. There was significant net outmigration. Industrial production and trade lagged. While a large number of new manufacturing establishments were started in this period, they were small, unspecialized and not very efficient. Politically, however, the National Policy helped to establish a nation and to determine that it would *remain* a nation. In short, its primary significance was not economic but political. And much of Canada's economic history over the past century was determined on a political rather than an economic basis, not unusual in the history of nations as parallels in the United States during the preceeding century demonstrate.

In the 1900s, the Canadian course of development continued to be halting and slow. It could not readily match the progress in England and other European nations. It had particular difficulty in keeping pace with the rate of U.S. industrial development, especially in light of the many advantages inherent in the U.S. pioneering of manufacturing and in the relatively much greater size and density of U.S. markets. Certain events, such as World War I, gave some Canadian industries special impetus. But the Great Depression was a withering experience for Canadian industry, relieved only in part by incentives to foreign corporations to establish or expand manufacturing operations in Canada behind a high tariff wall and to take advantage of preferential tariff access to Commonwealth markets, thus fostering selective aspects of Canadian industrial development.

However, Canada's significant role as one of the "arsenals of democracy" during World War II enhanced Canadian industrial capacities in a number of new ways, leading, for example, to the expansion and development of the aluminum, rubber, aircraft, uranium, shipbuilding, steel, and other industries. Moreover, many of these wartime initiatives were translated by astute postwar reconstruction policies and programs into measures to reshape Canadian industry and to capitalize on opportunities that would both serve domestic markets more effectively and develop an efficient export-orientation for many industries and product lines in a world dislocated and lacking capital and consumer goods. In brief, the Canadian economy moved from an agricultural and natural resource production base to strong positions in many basic industries, in the more sophisticated stages of natural resource processing, and in the production of much more technologically advanced products.

These developments rested on many complex factors. It is enough to say here that they laid the basis for Canada to move forward to achieve further manufacturing advances. These postwar successes and Canada's large involvement in, and contribution to, postwar rehabilitation and reconstruction in Europe and elsewhere encouraged strong national aspirations for the country to become a world industrial power.

After a decade of postwar development, however, new international realities began to limit Canadian progress. These issues were substantially sharpened during the late 1950s and early '60s when the Canadian economy encountered a period of slow economic growth, compounded by balance-of-payments and exchange-rate problems, high unemployment and concern about large, rapidly growing foreign investment and control of Canadian industries. It was in these circumstances that fundamental discussions about the nature and effectiveness of industrial strategies emerged as a powerful catalyst in the development of the issues and actions with which the remainder of this study is primarily concerned.

Thus, the issues dominating the current industrial policy debate are by no means new to Canada. Historically, they have played key roles in its development as a nation, especially in the twentieth century when industrial progress has often been perceived as the preferred course of development at the federal and provincial levels. In this context, the remarkably loose sharing of "sovereignties" between these governments has had, and will continue to have, a large role in the shaping of Canadian industrial policies.

We start this study, then, with the view that industrial policies have been threaded throughout the whole of Canada's economic development, but that events before the 1960s are essentially a prologue. It is the economic concerns since that time, and their meaning for the future, that we seek to define and clarify in the discussion that follows.

2

Economic Development Concerns
and Actions during the 1960s and 1970s

Over the past two decades, Canadians have been increasingly concerned about the adequacy of their economy's performance. Doubts have emerged about Canada's international competitiveness in the industrial sector and about the consistency of present paths and patterns of development in relation to Canadian political, social and cultural conditions and aspirations. At times, the focus has been on external relationships and Canada's place in the changing international environment. More generally, however, worries have centered on domestic conditions: capacity for growth—e.g., the adequacy of financing, markets, technological progress, manpower quality and deployment, and labor-management relations—and the quality of economic progress— e.g., the patterns of industrial and regional distribution of new employment opportunities.

These concerns initially emerged in a significant way at the beginning of the 1960s and substantially influenced domestic and international economic policy in several important areas: the magnitude and nature of government intervention in the economy, foreign investment and international trade.

During the 1950s, a minimum of institutions existed for government intervention or participation in the economy. Canada was open to foreign direct investment and played a leading role in encouraging an open trading system through the General Agreement on Tariffs and Trade (GATT) multilateral negotiations. Like other major industrial countries, Canada entered the postwar era with high levels of tariff protection, by today's standards, but was committed to a process of achieving freer trade through reciprocal tariff reductions and a more open payments system, a commitment implicit in its international and domestic economic policies.

CHANGING CONDITIONS

During the 1960s and '70s, several internal and external economic factors caused a gradual reevaluation of Canada's basic approach to economic and industrial development.

First, in the 1960s, Canada's growth performance was adequate. Real GNP grew at 5.2 percent annually, about the average of the other six leading industrial countries (see Table 1). But this record was achieved only because Canada's employment expansion (over 3 percent a year) was much greater than that of the other major industrial countries (see Table 2). Productivity growth in Canada was slower than that in most of the other industrial countries, and during the 1970s slowed significantly further and has been approximately zero since 1973.

Second, the persistence of disparities in regional economic performances focused attention on regional participation in and contribution to the national economy. Through the 1960s and '70s, earned personal income per capita and per employee in

TABLE 1. AVERAGE ANNUAL RATES OF REAL GNP GROWTH IN THE MAJOR INDUSTRIAL COUNTRIES, 1960–80 (Percent)

	1960–70	1970–80	1973–80
CANADA	5.2	4.1	3.0
United States	3.9	3.3	2.6
Germany	4.7	2.4	2.0
France	5.6	3.4	2.6
Italy	5.5	2.6	2.3
United Kingdom	2.9	1.5	1.0
Japan	11.1	4.9	3.6

Source: St. Louis Federal Reserve Bank, *International Economic Conditions* (various issues).

TABLE 2. AVERAGE ANNUAL GROWTH RATES OF PRODUCTIVITY AND EMPLOYMENT IN THE MAJOR INDUSTRIAL COUNTRIES, 1963–80 (Percent)

	Employment	
	1963–73	1973–80
CANADA	3.3	2.7
United States	2.2	2.1
Germany	0.0	– 0.6
France	0.9	0.1
Italy	– 0.6	0.9
United Kingdom	– 0.1	– 0.3
Japan	1.4	0.8
Average	1.1	1.1

	Productivity	
	1963–73	1973–80
CANADA	2.4	0.0
United States	1.9	0.1
Germany	4.6	2.9
France	4.6	2.5
Italy	5.4	1.9
United Kingdom	3.0	0.7
Japan	8.7	3.3
Average	3.8	1.4

Source: OECD, *Economic Outlook* (Paris, July 1980 and December 1981).

Quebec and the Atlantic provinces lagged behind national averages, while the opposite was true for unemployment rates.

Third, there was swiftly growing realization that Canada's extraordinarily high birth rate from the mid-1940s to the end of the '50s would lead to a rapidly expanding labor force, supported by a significant amount of net immigration, beginning in the 1960s. Thus, many new jobs would be needed to keep unemployment at relatively low levels. This contributed to a general concern about the economy's capacity to generate the quantity and quality of employment opportunities consistent with the aspirations of Canada's people, especially its youth.

There was also rapidly growing recognition of the inadequacies in Canada's educational efforts, including skilled training, manpower and human resource development. Into the 1960s, Canada depended heavily on postwar immigration to supply many types of blue- and white-collar technical workers. This led to large and costly efforts in some of the provinces to develop for the first time post-secondary technical training institutions.

Fourth, international competitive conditions intensified as the reconstructed European and Japanese economies became important competitors in areas dominated by North American firms after the destruction of World War II. Competitive pressures faced by Canada were also heightened by the freeing of trade through successive rounds of multilateral trade negotiations and the formation of the European Community and the European Free-Trade Association. The merging of these European markets left Canada as one of the few modern economies without open access to the large and protected markets that provide the basis for specialization and economies of scale in product development and production.

During the 1960s and '70s, Canada, like the United States and Northern Europe, experienced intensified competitive pressures in traditional manufacturing sectors (e.g., textiles, clothing and footwear) from countries with cheaper labor. In addition, Canadian industry was less productive and more in need of rationalization in certain sectors, such as automobiles, than industry in other major industrial countries.

Fifth, the opening of trade and the freeing of capital flows (by the postwar international monetary system), along with the growing importance of the rapid development, application and dissemination of technological advances, helped create a favorable climate for the growth of large multinational corporations in Canada. MNCs, in turn, became important vehicles for the expansion of trade, capital and technological flows. Their increasing power, however, was perceived by some as exerting considerable influence over the location of production and employment opportunities and the content and character of trade.

In these circumstances, Canada found itself in a rather ambivalent position. On the one hand, it had already developed a major industrial capacity that could benefit significantly from a more open world economy—if the necessary industrial rationalization and structural adjustment were accomplished. On the other hand, many Canadians began to feel that the other industrial economies were overtaking Canadian industry generally and that the relatively greater industrial development role that Canada had enjoyed after World War II was waning.

In this context, several problems became more prominent:

- Canada's lack of tariff-free access to a large and concentrated market, as existed within the United States and Japan and was emerging within Europe;

- the fragmented, overdiversified and uncompetitive manufacturing structure that had developed behind the tariff wall;

- the high degree of foreign ownership and control of Canadian industry and the growing questions about whether Canada's national interests—including its industrial development aspirations—would be adequately served by such a structure of ownership;

- the long-run competitive consequences of Canada's low levels of privately financed industrial R&D; and

• the general economic and political implications of Canada's dependence on the United States for investment funds and as a trading partner.

In addition to these largely economic problems, political, social and cultural developments emerged during the 1960s and '70s that over time significantly influenced the economic policy environment. These included growing constitutional problems characterized by federal-provincial rivalries; pressures for social programs to provide a more equitable distribution of income; rapid urbanization; growing cultural awareness and assertiveness among French Canadians; and increased concerns about Canadian cultural dependence on the United States. The latter encouraged greater emphasis on Canadian cultural and historical traditions and on more diversification of Canada's external relationships through closer ties with other countries, especially in Europe.

These economic and noneconomic developments together began to generate the basis for an enormous, but not totally coherent, set of actions intended to affect both specific and general adjustments in Canada's economic and, particularly, industrial structure. Three distinct elements characterized this process. First, new institutions were established to focus on matters of special concern. Second, a large number of programs were implemented to promote or protect certain industrial activities. Third, there was an extensive shift in the decisionmaking processes of government as they related to industrial policy.

INSTITUTIONAL CHANGE

Two philosophical or intellectual developments were important in the area of institutional change.

First, there was a gradual buildup of ideas and concepts to encourage or require foreign-owned firms in Canada to operate in ways contributing to the national goals of the country. This activity originated in two events in 1957: the report of the Royal Commission on Canada's Economic Prospects, chaired by Walter Gordon and known as the Gordon Report, and a key speech in Chicago by C.D. Howe, then Minister of Trade and Commerce. This interest subsequently led to a series of voluntary guidelines for foreign subsidiaries in Canada, issued in 1966 by the Minister of Trade and Commerce, Robert Winters, and then to a sequence of special federal and provincial studies conducted between 1968 and 1972. The institutional product of all this activity was the Foreign Investment Review Agency (FIRA), established in 1973 to screen proposals to increase foreign investment via takeovers or new projects (described in detail in Chapter 5).

Second, the Canadian approach toward trade liberalization began to change. During the late 1940s and '50s, Canada participated fully in the item-by-item tariff reductions negotiated in the early GATT rounds. But by the time of the Kennedy Round in the 1960s, Canada was playing a much less important part, and indeed made fewer and smaller tariff adjustments in the negotiations than did the United States and Western Europe for fear that it could not adjust as easily to substantial across-the-board tariff reductions.

Canada also displayed a willingness to use protectionist devices and production inducements to support some sectors adversely affected by trade and to manage the effects of freer trade to ensure results consistent with Canadian industrial aspirations.[1] The exchange of duty remission for increased production in the automotive sector in 1962 and 1963 and the performance requirements negotiated into the Canada-U.S. Automotive Agreement of 1965 are evidence of this inclination. (Appendix 1 provides a brief history of Canadian policy with respect to the automotive sector that culminated in the Automotive Agreement.)

Paralleling these changes in perceptions and policy was an extraordinary amount of institutional change—i.e., the proliferation of new institutions, such as FIRA, with terms of reference to assess and make recommendations regarding many different dimensions of Canadian economic and industrial development.

- Beginning around 1960, there was a rapid increase in the establishment of national and provincial economic and social advisory groups. At the federal level, these included the National Productivity Council in 1961, followed by the Economic Council of Canada with wider terms of reference in 1963. The Science Secretariat within the Cabinet Privy Council Office led to the development of the Science Council of Canada in 1966 and later to the establishment of the Ministry of State for Science and Technology in 1971. Similarly, at the provincial level many new agencies were established, such as the Manitoba Development Corporation (1958), the Quebec Economic Advisory Council (1961), the New Brunswick Research and Productivity Council (1962), and the Ontario Economic Council (1962).

- Also, there were major federal departmental extensions and reorganizations. For example, the Department of Industry was established in 1963; the Federal Department of Manpower and Immigration in 1966; the Department of Regional Economic Expansion (DREE) in 1969; various special ministries of state relating to the environment and urban affairs; and, much later, the Ministry of State for Economic Development in 1978. Other departments were substantially reorganized. For instance, the principal parts of the older Department of Natural Resources and Northern Development were shifted to become the Department of Energy, Mines and Resources in 1966. And in 1969, in an effort to establish greater coordination, especially regarding industrial development and commercial affairs, the Department of Industry was amalgamated with the Department of Trade and Commerce to form the Department of Industry, Trade, and Commerce (ITC). This department and DREE played important roles in implementing Canada's industrial policy programs until they were desolved in 1982.

Thus, the 1960s and '70s saw substantial growth and change in those governmental institutions intended to influence patterns of industrial development. The process appears to be continuing in the 1980s. In January 1982, the Liberal government announced a major restructuring of the federal departments most active in industrial policymaking and implementation in an effort to strengthen the regional and export development components of its industrial policies.

---

1   Emphasis should be placed on *some* sectors, because this was certainly not an across-the-board policy.

• The Cabinet Committee on Economic Development was renamed the Cabinet Committee on Economic and Regional Development. Its supporting secretariat was renamed the Ministry of State for Economic and Regional Development as it is to play a much larger role in the coordination and formulation of regional policy. For example, it was announced that the ministry will open regional offices in each province to ensure that regional concerns receive adequate consideration in industrial policymaking and budgeting decisions.

• The Department of Regional Industrial Expansion was formed by amalgamating most of DREE's program responsibilities with ITC's domestic industrial development, small business and tourism programs.

• The Department of External Affairs (headed by the Secretary of State for External Affairs) absorbed the export promotion programs formally administered by ITC, and the supervision of the Export Development Corporation and the Canadian Commercial Corporation was also transferred to the External Affairs portfolio. These actions and others centralize most export promotion activities along with other major international trade policymaking responsibilities under the supervision of External Affairs and its Secretary of State. It was also announced that a Minister for International Trade will assist the Secretary of State for External Affairs with these international trade policy and program responsibilities.

NEW PROGRAMS

Similarly, many new programs were put in place to improve the climate for industrial development by enhancing productivity, resolving structural problems within particular sectors and reducing regional disparities in economic performance and well-being. In the process, the Canadian government's intervention in the economic sphere expanded. It is important to note here that several major institutional activities and programs predate the 1960s. For example, the Export Credit Insurance Corporation was established in 1944 and reorganized into the Export Development Corporation in 1970. The Industrial Development Bank was also established in 1944 as a subsidiary of the Bank of Canada and in 1975 was entirely restructured into a separate Crown corporation, the Federal Business Development Bank. The Prairie Farm Rehabilitation Act Program, established in 1935 under the Department of Agriculture, was absorbed into DREE in 1969 as part of a special-area program. The federal government instituted a federal equalization payments system in 1957 to redistribute tax revenues from provinces with high taxing capacities.

Among the numerous new programs set up in the 1960s and '70s were:

• Program for the Advancement of Industrial Technology (PAIT), 1965;
• Industry Research and Development Incentives Act, 1965–75;
• Machinery Program, 1968;
• General Adjustment Assistance Program (GAAP), 1968;
• Pharmaceutical Industry Development Program (PIDP), 1968;
• Program to Enhance Productivity (PEP), 1970;
• Program for Export Market Development, 1971;
• Industrial Design Assistance Program (IDAP), 1971;
• Fashion Design Assistance Program, 1971;

- Footwear Tanning and Adjustment Program (FTAP), 1973;
- Promotional Projects Program, 1974;
- Shipbuilding Industry Assistance Program, 1975;
- Enterprise Development Program (replaced or absorbed the activities of PAIT, GAAP, PIDP, PEP, IDAP, and FTAP), 1977.

These programs were accompanied by other special arrangements and initiatives, such as the Defense Production Sharing Agreement with the United States (1958), and the Canada-U.S. Automotive Agreement (1965), an expansion of government ownership of firms in the resource processing and manufacturing sector, and more attention to "buy Canadian" in government procurement.

The federal government also experimented with several initiatives to reduce regional disparities in economic development:

- Agricultural and Rural Development Act, 1961;
- Atlantic Development Board, 1962;
- Area Development Act, 1963;
- Fund for Rural Economic Development, 1966;
- Cape Breton Development Corporation, 1967.

Many of these activities were absorbed by or put under supervision of DREE when it was created in 1969.

CHANGES IN GOVERNMENTAL STRUCTURES
AND DECISIONMAKING PROCESSES

In addition to the emergence of new institutions and programs that signaled an erosion of laissez-faire principles, important changes were taking place in the decision-making structures and processes within the existing governmental system. These are difficult to set forth in detail, partly because the changes depended much on subtleties not readily susceptible to description, partly because many different personalities were involved, and partly because few of the records that would illuminate these changes are in the public domain.

During the early 1960s, decisions concerning the development of new, or the extension of existing, programs and agency responsibilities were primarily generated by the Cabinet, whose considerations were based on the often rather piecemeal information presented to it. Then as now, the Minister and Department of Finance are responsible for advising the Cabinet on overall macro fiscal considerations, such as taxes, expenditures and debt financing. At the micro level, the Treasury Board—a Cabinet committee supported by a secretariat—reviews the activities of the various departments and agencies in terms of their effectiveness, efficiency, resource requirements, and so forth. However, until 1966, the Treasury Board Secretariat was located in the Department of Finance. Under these conditions, Finance was the real policymaking department within the Canadian federal structure, as it had been since the 1930s when it emerged as a pivotal policy center.

As economic and other affairs grew much more complex and intricate, especially by the late 1950s and '60s, Cabinet meetings became long and fairly contentious, sometimes dealing with matters in which few ministers had special interest or knowledge. To sort out some of these issues before they came to the Cabinet for decision, Prime Minister Lester Pearson set up, toward the end of the 1960s, four Cabinet policy planning committees, although these had little autonomy.

A further evolution in this direction occurred after Prime Minister Pierre Trudeau came into office in 1968. He established a Priorities and Planning Committee (P and P) of the Cabinet as a central committee to define priorities for the government based on a planning and systems approach and within the framework of overall policy and political considerations. P and P was served by the increased analytical capabilities of the Privy Council Office and to have greater power and autonomy than the other Cabinet committees. This effort to better set priorities and define policies became what Richard French has called the Cabinet Planning System.[2]

When Douglas Hartle became Deputy Secretary for Planning at the Treasury Board in 1969, he began to undertake far more intensive technical appraisals of the individual departmental and agency programs by using what were then considered advanced quantitative analytical techniques, such as program budgeting.[3] This process moved forward with great vigor and with a growing cadre of well trained personnel, even though it met with much opposition from some of the entrenched bureaucracy. French has characterized this effort as the Treasury Planning System.

The Treasury and Cabinet Planning Systems and the Financial Planning System, which had developed over the years in the Department of Finance, came into direct competition with each other. Considerable contention and confusion appears to have developed between the three planning systems, but the Cabinet Planning System eventually prevailed and became the central system for federal decisionmaking processes.

In the Cabinet Planning System that emerged at the end of the seventies, P and P sets the government's overall priorities, but delegates a great deal of authority for achieving these objectives to Cabinet committees. The system has considerable importance for the future of Canadian industrial policy. It provides what has been sorely lacking in the past: a vehicle for coordinating the large number of federal programs and institutions affecting economic development that emerged out of the concerns of the 1960s and '70s. This planning system is the focus of the next chapter.

---

2   Richard French, How Ottawa Decides: Planning and Industrial Policy-Making 1968–1980 (Ottawa: Canadian Institute for Economic Policy, 1980).

3   At around the same time, similar reappraisals of government decisionmaking processes focusing on efficiency and effectiveness were proceeding in a number of the provinces. Perhaps the most notable of these was an exercise sponsored by the government of Ontario, which produced a report in 1970 on The Management of Government: An Appraisal, followed by six reports under a Committee on Government Productivity examining in some detail many of the processes for more efficient governmental decisionmaking in that province.

3

Further Cabinet Reforms
and the Industrial Policymaking Process

During his relatively short term as Prime Minister from June 1979 to March 1980, Joe Clark continued the process of delegating policymaking responsibility to Cabinet committees. Further, he established a Policy and Expenditure Management System, which represented the culmination of the evolutionary process begun in the Pearson/Trudeau years and which Trudeau maintained upon returning to power. Clark also continued the Trudeau innovation of a strong central planning committee, setting up an Inner Cabinet that was in many ways the analogue to Trudeau's Planning and Priorities Committee. The IC retained only a limited degree of final decisionmaking authority, a far cry from the days when the full Cabinet alone would make all basic decisions on major policy issues. Indeed, by this time, a significant degree of the decisionmaking responsibility appears to have been delegated to the policy committees. The important committee from an industrial policy perspective, the Board of Economic Development Ministers, and its supporting secretariat, the Ministry of State for Economic Development, were carried over from the Trudeau government that ended in 1979. Clark's new Economic Development Committee inherited the responsibilities of that Board and its secretariat, as well as the activities of Trudeau's Economic Policy Committee. Upon returning to power in 1980, Trudeau retained the Economic Development Committee and in 1982 renamed it the Cabinet Committee on Economic and Regional Development (CCERD).

The Cabinet Planning System now in place has two important elements. First, it establishes, more or less, two tiers of policymaking responsibility. A small group, P and P (upon reassuming power, Trudeau again adopted the name Priorities and Planning Committee for his central policymaking committee), sets overall policy objectives for the government and expenditure guidelines for the various policy areas, while responsibility for formulating specific policies and programs to achieve these objectives is delegated to the policy committees. Second, it establishes a Policy and Expenditure Management System, often called the Envelope System, that effectively makes this cabinet structure a key element in governmental planning.

As noted in Chapter 2, prior to the Envelope System the Minister of Finance had primary responsibility, in consultation with the Treasury Board, for setting overall expenditure targets. Each minister or agency head would transmit a proposed budget to the Treasury Board, which would recommend appropriate expenditure levels to Finance, based on efficiency and effectiveness criteria. In effect, each department and agency had to bargain with the Treasury Board for its programs. Therefore, the Board played a major role in allocating resources in a manner that reflected the government's overall fiscal constraints and priorities.[1]

---

1   The Treasury Board had the particularly important power and responsibility of setting the numbers and levels of personnel in all departments and agencies.

The Envelope System embodies two fundamental reforms:

- the preparation and publication of a multiyear plan for government revenues and expenditures;

- the division of expenditures into policy sectors, or envelopes, the establishment of specific expenditure limits for each envelope, and the delegation of the management of the policies and expenditures within each envelope to a policy committee.[2]

Under the new budget process, the P and P, with the aid of its secretariat the Privy Council Office, sets overall expenditure levels for the entire government and individual policy sectors. As principal financial advisers to the government, the Minister of Finance and the President of the Treasury Board provide recommendations and analyses that assist in this process. P and P also outlines the government's priorities and transmits these to the various policy committees. These committees seek to forge their individual policies and programs into a *common government approach* within the policy sector. The policy committees make specific directives to the departments who draw up budgets and submit proposed program expenditures to their policy committees and the Treasury Board. Proposed budgets are then modified to conform to the policy committee's expenditure constraints and priorities. In this process, ministers with programs in the same policy areas must together justify their expenditures and allocate funds among competing uses. P and P may override a policy committee's decision, but this is not expected to occur often, since the Prime Minister clearly wishes the committee to exercise fiscal responsibility and restraint. The committee structure and the responsibilities of P and P, Department of Finance, Treasury Board, and policy committees are illustrated in Figure 1.

The system requires the ministers on a policy committee to give adequate consideration to the programs of other departments and to know how much the government can afford to devote to each broad policy area when drafting program budgets and proposing new expenditure initiatives. To the extent that policy committees create new programs, the resources must be found within their own envelopes. It places the responsibility for pruning budgets and staying within them on the shoulders of those who spend the money. Further, to the extent that policy committees propose tax incentives, these tax expenditures (losses), if approved, come out of their envelopes. Also, policy committees are expected to give full consideration to the various nonexpenditure policy tools, such as regulations, in planning their programs.

The CCERD, chaired by the Minister of State for Economic and Regional Development, manages the economic and regional development and energy envelopes, which, as of early 1982, included 21 of the 36 Cabinet members, almost everyone managing a program with an impact on economic development.[3] The departments and agencies requiring annual budgetary allocations from these two envelopes are listed in Figure 2.

The CCERD closely monitors their policies and expenditures. On a weekly basis, virtually all individual policy and expenditure proposals are submitted to the CCERD

---

2   Each policy committee manages two envelopes.

3   Although the CCERD is responsible for managing economic development policy and allocating funds earmarked for economic development, it is not responsible for Canadian macro fiscal or monetary policies.

FIGURE 1. CABINET POLICY COMMITTEE STRUCTURE AND POLICY COMMITTEE RESOURCE ENVELOPES

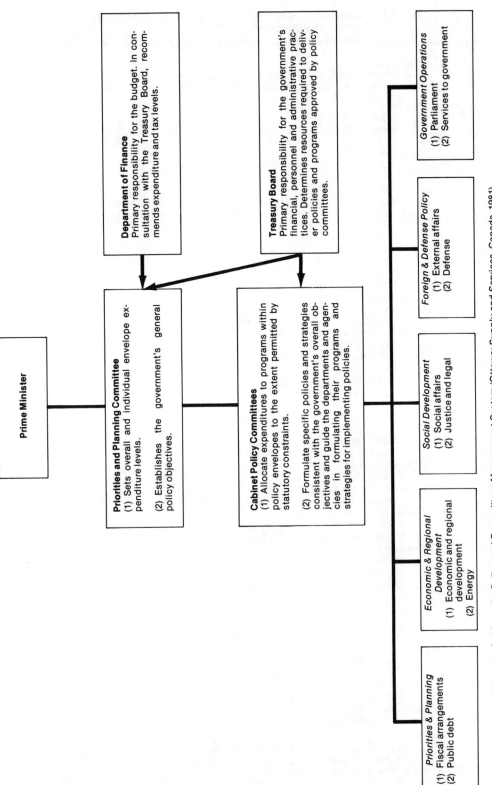

Prime Minister

Priorities and Planning Committee
(1) Sets overall and individual envelope expenditure levels.

(2) Establishes the government's general policy objectives.

Department of Finance
Primary responsibility for the budget. In consultation with the Treasury Board, recommends expenditure and tax levels.

Treasury Board
Primary responsibility for the government's financial, personnel and administrative practices. Determines resources required to deliver policies and programs approved by policy committees.

Cabinet Policy Committees
(1) Allocate expenditures to programs within policy envelopes to the extent permitted by statutory constraints.

(2) Formulate specific policies and strategies consistent with the government's overall objectives and guide the departments and agencies in formulating their programs and strategies for implementing policies.

Priorities & Planning
(1) Fiscal arrangements
(2) Public debt

Economic & Regional Development
(1) Economic and regional development
(2) Energy

Social Development
(1) Social affairs
(2) Justice and legal

Foreign & Defense Policy
(1) External affairs
(2) Defense

Government Operations
(1) Parliament
(2) Services to government

Source: Government of Canada, *Guide to the Policy and Expenditure Management System* (Ottawa: Supply and Services Canada, 1981).

**FIGURE 2. CABINET COMMITTEE ON ECONOMIC AND REGIONAL
DEVELOPMENT ENVELOPES
Departments and Agencies Requiring Annual Appropriations**

A. Economic and Regional Development Envelope
(Department and agencies listed by responsible ministers*)

Agriculture
  Department of Agriculture
  Canadian Dairy Commission
  Canadian Livestock Feed Board
Communications
  Department of Communications
Consumer and Corporate Affairs
Economic and Regional Development
  Ministry of State for Economic and Regional Development—provides
    secretariat services to the Cabinet Committee on Economic and
    Regional Development
Energy, Mines and Resources
  Part of Department of Energy, Mines and Resources—Minerals and
    Earth Sciences
Environment
  Part of Department of Environment—Forestry
External Affairs
  Export Development Corporation
  Canadian Commercial Corporation
Fisheries and Oceans
  Department of Fisheries and Oceans
Regional Industrial Expansion
  Department of Regional Industrial Expansion
  Federal Business Development Bank
  Foreign Investment Review Agency
  Standards Council of Canada
  Cape Breton Development Corporation
Labor
  Department of Labor
  Canadian Labor Relations Board
Science and Technology
  Ministry of State for Science and Technology
  National Research Council
  Natural Sciences and Engineering Council
Supply and Services Canada
  Part of Department of Supply and Services
    Canada—Unsolicited R&D proposals
Transport
  Department of Transport
  Air Canada
  Canadian Transport Commission

B. Energy Envelope

Energy, Mines and Resources
  Part of Department of Energy, Mines and Resources—Energy,
    Petroleum Compensation Program, Sarnia-Montreal Pipeline, Cana-
    dian Home Insulation Program
  Atomic Energy Control Board
  National Energy Board
  PetroCan
Economic and Regional Development
  Northern Pipeline Agency

*Agencies report to Parliament through designated ministers.
Sources: Government of Canada, *Guide to the Policy and Expenditure Management
System* (Ottawa: Supply and Services Canada, 1981) and Office of the Prime Minister,
press release, January 12, 1982.

for consideration and decision after they have been prescreened by a committee of deputy ministers. The weekly agenda may cover a wide range of items, including, for example, consideration of financial assistance to modernize a paper mill and discussion of the future of Canada's natural resource policy.

The Minister of State for Economic and Regional Development is not responsible for the management or implementation of any particular program but rather for encouraging general coordination of economic development programs into an approach consistent with the government's objectives. He is assisted by a secretariat, the Ministry of State for Economic and Regional Development. As chairman of this important policy committee, the minister, with the support of the MSERD, is responsible for leading the process of policy development within the CCERD, for providing it with the information, technical and otherwise, necessary to evaluate the tradeoffs among the various departments' alternative programs, and for analyzing the programs that require discretionary funds or policy changes. Hence, the minister plays a significant role in encouraging the coordination and harmonization of programs. It should be stressed, however, that the minister and the CCERD receive guidance from P and P about the government's priorities and desired tone for economic development policy. The minister and the CCERD may also receive similar guidance from special ad hoc committees of the Cabinet, such as the group chaired by Finance Minister MacEachen during the summer of 1981 that drafted *Economic Development for Canada in the 1980s*, which outlined some general policy goals for economic development. In addition, the minister's responsibilities do not preclude cooperative efforts with departments or substantial initiatives by other ministers and departments in the framing of economic development policy. For example, Herb Gray, Minister of Regional Industrial Expansion, has made efforts to define an overall framework for an explicit Canadian industrial policy in recent years.

The government's ability to restructure its programs affecting industrial development depends in large part on the ability of the CCERD, or one of its key members, to frame a new *explicit* industrial policy. This will in turn depend on the CCERD's ability to achieve a working consensus and formulate a politically acceptable statement of industrial policy goals and programs. Given the many divergent views about the appropriate goals and means for Canadian industrial policy, both inside and outside the government, it is no easy task. It may never be possible to forge in Canada the kinds of detailed government-directed approaches to industrial development pursued in Japan and France at various times over the last several decades.

Nevertheless, the CCERD has functioned well in keeping its expenditures within the designated envelope levels. With the assistance of the MSERD, it provides the ministers with a vehicle for analyzing the overall long-range effects of programs and policies on the evolution of Canada's industrial structure and for modifying them when the outcome is perceived to be undesirable. Therefore, initiatives to coordinate programs in a better fashion, making them more effective and responsive to Canada's industrial policy objectives, may be possible even if radical new departures are not politically feasible.

In moving in this direction, the CCERD and the Cabinet are faced with many constraints. Chapter 4 examines these within the context of Canada's industrial policy objectives.

4

Canadian Industrial Policy Objectives and Constraints

As noted in Chapter 2, Canada, like other major industrial countries, emerged from World War II with high tariffs. It became a strong advocate of the GATT process and participated in multilateral tariff reductions on a full basis through the early 1960s. Nevertheless, it entered the 1970s with higher average levels of protection than many other major industrial economies (see Table 3[1]), in part because of its less than full participation in the Kennedy Round across-the-board tariff reductions. More important, though, Canada's tariffs have been high enough throughout this century to encourage the production of a much greater range and selection of manufactured products—and the establishment of many foreign subsidiaries for that purpose—than would have been the case if Canada had been more open to imports. Combined with Canada's small population, this has led to a fragmented and overdiversified structure of production. Many foreign firms produce in Canada essentially for the Canadian market, and maintain product development, international marketing and other major functional responsibilities in their home countries.

During the 1970s, there was a growing realization that this situation could not continue. The Tokyo Round tariff cuts will substantially reduce, and for some areas essentially remove, Canada's tariff wall, compelling Canadian manufacturers to rationalize. The pressure created by increased competition will add to current account problems if Canadian industry does not adjust to meet this competition and exploit new export opportunities created by reciprocal tariff concessions. Given the enormous importance of trade to Canada, a major restructuring of Canadian industry will be required to overcome these problems.

TABLE 3. AVERAGE TARIFFS[1] FOR INDUSTRIAL PRODUCTS,[2] 1973

	All Imports	Dutiable Items Only
Canada	9.9	13.1
United States	6.1	8.2
Japan	3.2	6.9
EC	6.3	9.8

[1]Import weighted average applied tariff rates.
[2]All manufacturing, except food, tobacco and petroleum products.
Source: Office of the Special Trade Representative, *Results of the United States Industrial Tariff Negotiations with Other Major Industrial Countries in the Multilateral Trade Negotiations* (Washington, D.C., June 21, 1979).

---

1   The comparisons for tariffs on dutiable imports only are particularly important because they exclude the influence of tariff free trade in automobiles between the United States and Canada. However, the conclusions obtained from comparing average tariffs must be viewed as approximate because the results of such analyses are sensitive to the weights employed in computing averages.

Since 1974, Canada's current account has been in deficit. Equally important, from 1974 to 1981, the value of the Canadian dollar declined substantially on foreign exchange markets—over 20 percent against the U.S. dollar. This depreciation did not reflect merely differential rates of inflation, as Canada's terms of trade on goods and services deteriorated by about 10 percent. Many Canadian's are concerned that the value of the Canadian dollar will slide still further in the years ahead, increasing inflation and the real cost of imports. Moreover, examination of various components of the current account indicate that long-term improvements are not likely without an improvement in Canada's competitive position through a restructuring of the manufacturing sector.

As Figure 3 illustrates, over the past two decades Canada has had a surplus on its merchandise trade account, but a continuously growing deficit on its services account. The latter grew from 2.5 percent of GNP in 1974 to 4.5 percent in 1981. The merchandise trade surplus has been generated by growing net exports of primary and semifabricated (manufactured) materials, while trade in finished manufactures has been in persistent deficit, about 6.3 percent of GNP in both 1974 and 1981.

Unfortunately, Canada may not be able to count on enough growth in its natural resource-based exports of primary and semifabricated materials to offset its growing deficits on the services account and in finished manufactures. If Australia, South

FIGURE 3. CANADA'S CURRENT ACCOUNT BALANCE, 1961–81

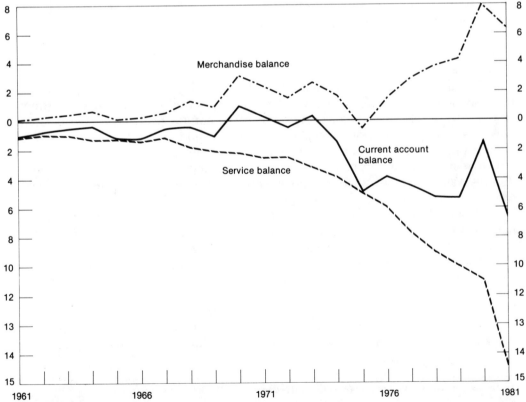

Sources: Department of Finance, *Economic Review* (Ottawa: Supply and Services Canada, 1981), Chart 5.1, p. 58, and *Bank of Canada Review* (March 1982).

Africa and other resource rich countries of the Third World effectively develop and promote their resource industries, many of which have large, high quality reserves, Canada could face sizable increased competition in world markets for natural resources and industrial materials. Today, Canada is an important exporter of basic resources such as nickel, zinc, asbestos, lead, copper, iron ore, forest products, fish, and grain. But potential alternative sources could erode Canada's position as an exporter of some of these commodities. Canada will probably have to invest in more downstream manufacturing and processing of resources and focus its investments in areas where substantial opportunities remain to maintain the large positive trade balance it enjoys in the natural resource-based sectors.

Further, Canada's current account difficulties are not likely to be eliminated by a dramatic improvement in the services account deficit. As Table 4 indicates, the majority of this deficit is derived from large and increasing net interest and dividend payments, although negative balances on travel and nontransportation services have also been growing.[2] These net interest and dividend payments will not abate in the future because (1) Canada has a sizable external debt, mainly denominated in U.S. dollars, and (2) the debt has been growing in recent years. Large Canadian securities issues have been the most important positive element in Canada's capital account offsetting its current account deficit.[3]

Therefore, efforts to reduce the growth of the current account deficit and halt the depreciation of the value of the Canadian dollar must, at the level of industrial policy, place adequate emphasis on improving the competitive position of Canadian manufacturing while, at the level of macro policy, focus on bringing inflation under control and improving general productivity growth.

POLICY OBJECTIVES

Canada's persistent current account problems and the anticipated implications of the reduction in Canadian tariffs through the 1980s, as well as the massive investments required to develop Canadian energy and other natural resources, have created a sense of urgency in many quarters about the need to address *finally* Canada's structural problems with a consistent set of economic development policies. This process will require reallocation of resources among sectors and increased specialization within industries. While there are sharp disagreements about appropriate approaches, there is some agreement about the desired objectives for such a policy.

Most observers believe Canada should continue to pursue its opportunities in the natural resource sectors, but it is an important and widely shared view that Canada must maximize the benefits it receives through the development of these resources. It should seek to increase the value added to these resources within Canada through further processing and secondary manufacturing before being exported, thereby expanding the quality and quantity of jobs created as well as enhancing Canada's export performance.

Also, many Canadians believe that Canada could play a larger role in the development, production and worldwide marketing of sophisticated, high technology goods

---

2   Throughout the study, financial data are expressed in Canadian dollars unless otherwise noted.

3   Specifically, from 1975 to 1980, net foreign issues of Canadian securities exceeded Canada's current account deficit by 20 percent. Net new issues were equal to 2.2 percent of GNP.

TABLE 4. CANADIAN SERVICES ACCOUNT BALANCE, 1970–81
      ($ Can. Millions)

	Interest and Dividends	Freight and Shipping	Travel	Other	Total
1970	− 1,022	20	− 216	− 881	− 2,099
1971	− 1,141	− 12	− 202	− 1,043	− 2,398
1972	− 1,048	− 74	− 234	− 1,171	− 2,527
1973	− 1,260	− 66	− 296	− 1,349	− 2,971
1974	− 1,553	− 224	− 284	− 1,645	− 3,706
1975	− 1,953	− 433	− 727	− 1,573	− 4,686
1976	− 2,498	− 150	− 1,191	− 1,921	− 5,760
1977	− 3,658	− 26	− 1,641	− 2,119	− 7,444
1978	− 4,499	130	− 1,706	− 2,615	− 8,690
1979	− 5,299	290	− 1,068	− 3,655	− 9,732
1980	− 5,561	433	− 1,138	− 4,471	− 10,737
1981	− 6,982	243	− 1,158	− 6,917	− 14,814

Sources: Department of Finance, *Economic Review* (Ottawa: Supply and Services Canada, 1981), pp. 195, 198 and 199, and *Bank of Canada Review* (February 1982), Table 10.

and services.[4] Historically, Canada has been competitive in a few of these industries, where it has a strong base of experience from the development of its natural resources; but the share of GNP devoted to R&D in Canada has lagged behind other major industrial countries. Both the federal and provincial governments place a high priority on encouraging the development of high technology industries and on increasing indigenous basic research and product development efforts.

Closely related to the desire to develop high technology activities are aspirations concerning the way rationalization within sectors—the production of fewer products on longer production runs—takes place. Some Canadians, such as Larry Grossman, former Ontario Minister of Industry and Tourism, would like to see rationalization entail more than longer production runs and greater specialization. They would prefer that Canadian subsidiaries of MNCs receive "global product mandates"—that is, the subsidiaries would become responsible, on a selective basis by product lines, for all phases of product development, from design and testing to production to global marketing involving substantial exports.

Also, given the continuing problem of high unemployment, aspirations continue for projects and initiatives that could yield large and attractive employment opportunities. And it is strongly believed that employment opportunities and the benefits of economic development should be adequately shared by all of Canada's regions.

Finally, closely related to these industrial policy objectives is the view held by many—but not all—that Canada should reduce the control of foreign investors over its means of production, perhaps especially in its critical resource sectors.

CONSTRAINTS ON CANADIAN POLICYMAKERS

Like all nations, Canada uses a variety of measures to pursue its industrial policy goals. These tools, discussed in Chapter 5, may be divided into international trade poli-

---

4   In general, economists do not believe that Canada has an across-the-board comparative advantage in high technology, R&D-intense activities. However, there are important exceptions in areas where Canada has developed expertise through the development of its natural resource industries and from dealing with its great distances and climate—e.g., hydroelectric generation equipment, construction engineering, frontier energy exploration, and transportation equipment.

cies, which include import barriers and export promotion programs; and domestic policies, which provide special assistance to selected industries, labor-force groups and regions. However, in applying these tools, many constraints impede Canadian policymakers' efforts to achieve their industrial policy objectives.

(1) The slow growth expected for the rest of the 1980s in Canada[5] will increase pressures for measures to insulate workers from market forces and reduce Canada's latitude to encourage positive adjustment. Economic growth can lessen the dislocations and hardships imposed by structural change by permitting employment in adversely affected industries to decline in relative importance rather than in absolute size. However, the magnitude of structural change required in Canada, coupled with rates of growth that will likely continue below the levels of the 1960s, will probably not allow gradual adjustments without policy initiatives to reduce the rate of change that would be induced by market forces. To the extent that Canada yields to demands to lean against the forces of change to cushion economic hardships, some of the adjustment pressures will undoubtedly be transferred to the United States and Canada's other trading partners. The converse is also true.

(2) The denomination in U.S. dollars of interest and dividend payments, the large size of Canada's external debt and the desire to maintain Canadian living standards essentially preclude large *deliberate* exchange-rate adjustments as an industrial policy tool.

(3) Fiscal constraints are important. Canadian federal government deficits averaged close to 4 percent of GNP and about 25 percent of total revenues over the 1977–80 period (see Table 5). As in the United States, a substantial proportion of total expenditures are legislatively mandated (especially in the field of social programs and transfer payment systems) or are affected by events beyond fiscal policy control, such as payments of interest on the public debt. Therefore, resources for new programs to assist industrial development—in the form of direct expenditures or tax breaks—will

TABLE 5. CANADIAN FEDERAL SURPLUSES AND DEFICITS, 1973–80

	Revenue ($ Can. Millions)	Expenditure ($ Can. Millions)	Surplus or Deficit ($ Can. Millions)	Surplus or Deficit (Percent of GNP)
1973	22,809	22,422	387	0.3
1974	29,978	28,869	1,109	0.8
1975	31,703	35,508	− 3,805	2.3
1976	35,313	38,704	− 3,391	1.8
1977	36,214	43,807	− 7,593	3.6
1978	38,019	48,974	− 10,955	4.8
1979	43,518	52,649	− 9,131	3.5
1980	50,099	60,822	− 10,723	3.7

Source: Department of Finance, *Economic Review* (Ottawa: Supply and Services Canada, 1981), Table 6.1, p. 72.

5   In its latest projections for the Canadian economy, the Department of Finance assumes the U.S. economy will grow at a 2.6 percent average annual rate from 1981 to 1987. Canada's growth rate is projected to be 2.7 percent over the same period. Department of Finance, *The Current Economic Situation and Prospects for the Canadian Economy in the Short and Medium Term* (Ottawa, November 1981), pp. 11 and 19.

TABLE 6. COMPOSITION OF PROVINCIAL AND LOCAL NET BALANCES, 1973-80

| | Revenue | | Expenditure | | Surplus or deficit(-) | | |
					All provinces	Sask., Alta. & B.C.	Other provinces
	($m)	(per cent change)	($m)	(per cent change)	($m)	($m)	($m)
1973	26,420	14.1	27,024	13.1	−604	298	−902
1974	32,630	23.5	32,715	21.1	−85	799	−884
1975	37,426	14.7	39,673	21.3	−2,247	377	−2,624
1976	43,423	16.0	45,437	14.5	−2,014	935	−2,949
1977	50,983	17.4	51,044	12.3	−61	1,902	−1,963
1978	57,352	12.5	55,948	9.6	1,404	2,918	−1,514
1979	63,352	10.5	61,495	9.9	1,857	2,997	−1,140
1980	70,642	11.5	69,400	12.9	1,242	3,356	−2,114

Source: Reproduced from the Department of Finance, *Economic Review* (Ottawa: Supply and Services Canada, 1981), Table 6.7, p. 79.

be difficult to find unless the government raises sizable new taxes or reduces other spending. During 1980 and 1981, the government moved in this direction by implementing the National Energy Program, in which subsidies on imported oil are being phased out—freeing some $3 billion per year—and imposed additional energy taxes. Further, in the November 1981 Budget Speech, the government announced plans to increase income tax revenues. Although some of these revenues have already been moved to the economic and regional development envelope, the need to hold down spending overall and reduce the federal deficit essentially precludes the allocation of substantial new funds to this policy sector. And in 1982, this problem has been exacerbated by the impacts of the recession on federal revenues and expenditures.

As Table 6 shows, in recent years the combined budgets of the provincial and local governments are in approximate balance, but there is considerable regional imbalance in the resources available to provincial (and their respective local) governments. For much of the last decade, Saskatchewan, Alberta and British Columbia provincial and local governments experienced growing combined surpluses that were about 1.2 percent of GNP in 1980. In contrast, the rest of Canada's subnational governments had combined budget deficits that were about 0.7 percent of GNP in 1980. Therefore, the eastern provinces of Quebec and Ontario and the Atlantic region—where a great deal of rationalization and redeployment of resources are needed—will find it difficult to institute new or expand existing industrial assistance programs. Further, like that of the federal government, the fiscal positions of the provinces have been hurt by the recession.

(4) Canadian policymakers are constrained by GATT commitments, specifically elements of the new GATT codes governing the application of nontariff barriers (NTBs),[6] as well as the rights previously afforded Canada's trading partners. Similarly, Canada's participation in the Tokyo Round tariff cuts limits new initiatives in the commercial policy field for industrial policy purposes.

---

6 The codes cover government procurement, customs valuation, subsidies and countervailing duties, antidumping duties, product standards, and import licensing.

The code regarding government procurement will restrict the Canadian federal government's ability to discriminate in favor of selected firms, or Canadian suppliers in general, to encourage development. However, as discussed in Chapter 5, the government has sought ways to persuade private firms and Crown corporations to buy national. Further, since GATT codes regarding procurement do not apply to provincial and local governments, substantial use of this tool is likely to continue in the future at the provincial and local levels. The codes governing subsidies and countervailing duties, product standards and customs valuation should also limit, but certainly not eliminate, the use of NTBs in industrial policy.

The constraints on trade measures, coupled with the tight fiscal situation of many Canadian governments, could result in increased efforts to leverage private resources by both the federal and provincial levels. These initiatives aimed at influencing private business decisions include performance requirements for foreign investors and for firms seeking access to Canada's publicly owned natural resources. For example, the Foreign Investment Review Agency already reviews new foreign investments (including transfer of assets from one foreign MNC to another) and the expansion of existing facilities in terms of their contribution to Canadian industrial policy objectives (described in detail in Chapter 5).

(5) Many Canadians believe that industrial policy objectives in Canada are being constrained because decisions made by parent companies affecting manufacturing in foreign-owned subsidiaries reflect MNC global strategies rather than Canadian national industrial policy interests. In some sectors, rationalization schemes in which Canadian facilities would produce a few products for the entire North American market and provide distribution facilities for other products may seem more practical to the parent firms than granting the Canadian subsidiary a global product mandate for complete development and world marketing of one product, or a limited number of products. The reasons may be rooted in objective efficiency considerations, such as the belief that substantial externalities are possible in product development or world marketing when these activities are performed centrally for all product lines. Sometimes, however, such decisions may simply be the outcome of habit.

(6) A constraint closely related to foreign ownership is the extraterritorial application of U.S. laws on U.S. MNC activities in Canada. Under U.S. antitrust law, U.S. parent firms are accountable for the actions of a Canadian subsidiary that affect competition in U.S. markets, even if all production involved is located in Canada.

For example, during the late 1970s, Pratt and Whitney (United States) consulted the U.S. Justice Department about an intended $100 million joint venture between Pratt and Whitney (Canada) and Rolls-Royce to build small jet engines in Canada. This market is highly concentrated in the United States. The Justice Department determined that the joint venture was not necessary to permit the principals to enter the market and notified Pratt and Whitney of its intention to file suit if the venture was consummated. The deal was not completed.

Other U.S. laws can inhibit the activities of Canadian subsidiaries of U.S. MNCs, such as the U.S. Trading with the Enemy Act, U.S. foreign asset control regulations, U.S. financial regulations, and U.S. antiboycott measures. The external application of U.S. laws can impose a significant constraint on Canadian industrial policymakers and is a source of friction between the two countries.

(7) In pursuing its industrial policy objectives, Canada will be faced with trade-offs between its regional development commitments and the necessary restructuring and modernization of its industrial base. While Canada provides substantial assistance

and incentives for the relocation of labor, there is a persistent regional imbalance between employment opportunities and location of the labor force. This situation is reflected in chronic higher than average unemployment rates in Quebec and the Atlantic region. Cultural affinities in these regions, as well as federal redistribution programs—especially the federal equalization payments system—have contributed to this situation. Nevertheless, the federal government is committed to programs that ensure some regional sharing of Canada's overall economic progress. This policy may impede industrial development and structural adjustments by encouraging the maintenance and further establishment of an inefficient spatial distribution of Canadian industry and by absorbing federal resources that might be used to stimulate rationalization. However, the nature of this tradeoff is well perceived in Canada, and it appears that Canadians are willing to accept some sacrifice of economic efficiency to achieve regional objectives.

(8) Closely related to the preceeding constraint are the conflicts between federal and provincial development objectives. The provinces have established a variety of development corporations and export promotion programs and use many of the instruments of industrial policy to achieve their own development goals. While the Department of Regional Industrial Expansion's programs provide substantial federal resources that complement provincial programs, conflicts are common. There has been a rise in interprovincial barriers to trade, and the provinces increasingly have been asserting their intention to influence their own industrial development. This has generated concern within the federal government that its constitutional powers relating to national economic development, and therefore its ability to maintain a Canadian common market, are being challenged. A considerable constraint is thus imposed on the planning of a national industrial policy based on a national view of resource endowments and regional comparative advantages.

(9) Still another constraint is the shortage of certain types of labor, especially skilled technicians, in the northern and western regions and its potential for sharply accelerated rates of development. This situation is attributable in part to inadequate levels of east-west migration, inadequate skill-training programs and past reliance on immigration for skilled tradesworkers (now curtailed under the immigration policy of 1977).

The Economic Council of Canada recently conducted a Human Resources Survey of 1,354 firms in all regions and sectors of the economy.[7] The study indicates substantial shortages are present and likely to persist for many important types of highly skilled blue-collar workers and some categories of white-collar professional and technical workers. Shortages are particularly acute in the west, especially Alberta, but problems exist in each region. Consequently, greater labor mobility will not provide the full answer.

Shortages of skilled labor are affecting mining, manufacturing and construction, as well as other sectors, and are especially critical in product fabricating and repair—e.g., industrial machinery mechanics, motor vehicle mechanics and industrial electricians—and machinery skills—e.g., tool and die makers and welders. Also, there are shortages in many of the construction trades and in several white-collar groups—e.g., engineers, engineering technicians and some types of managerial personnel.[8]

---

7   Gordon Betcherman, *Skills and Shortages: A Summary Guide to the Findings of the Human Resources Survey* (Ottawa: Supply and Services Canada, 1980).

8   Ibid. and William Dodge, *Skilled Labor Supply Imbalances: The Canadian Experience* (Washington, D.C.: British-North American Committee, 1977).

Two factors may limit the availability of critical, highly skilled manpower over the next decade.

• The average age of industrial tradesworkers is relatively high, especially in the more heavily industrialized areas of eastern Canada, so retirements from the workforce will accelerate in the 1980s.

• The many new post-secondary technical training institutions established in the 1960s will be operating under significant financial constraints in the 1980s at the same time that the skilled training in these institutions will continue to be much more expensive than traditional academic schooling.

5

Current Canadian Programs

In the Introduction, industrial policy was defined to include those programs and policies designed to impact directly on the domestic and/or international competitiveness of firms and industries, the employment opportunities and incomes of segments of the labor force, and/or the development of selected regions. Industrial policy tools, when part of a coherent policy or initiative, are intended to influence (change) the evolution of the structure of the economy to achieve a more desired outcome.

The tools that may be employed to achieve industrial policy objectives are listed in Figure 4. They include international trade policies designed to protect domestic in-

FIGURE 4. INDUSTRIAL POLICY TOOLS

A. International Trade Policies

    Tariffs
    Nontariff barriers
      Quantitative restrictions
      Discriminatory government procurement
      Discriminatory applications of taxes, standards, regulations,
        industry incentives, etc.
      Others
    Export promotion
    Exchange-rate management

B. General Domestic Economic Policies

    Policies toward inward foreign direct investment
    Competition and antitrust policy
    Regulation
    General tax policy

C. Industry, Firm and Individual-Directed
Domestic Economic Policies

    Research and development incentives
    Direct and indirect financial incentives and assistance to firms
      Direct subsidies
      Intervention in capital markets
      Technical assistance
      Adjustment assistance to firms
      Small business assistance
      Tax policies—differential tax treatment
    Manpower policies (including adjustment assistance to employees)
    Research and development assistance
    Government procurement
    Public ownership
    Regional policies

dustries from foreign competition and to make exports more attractive, such as below-market export-credit financing, export subsidies and government-financed marketing programs. There are also many domestic policy tools that favor some industries at the expense of others, including general policies that affect the overall economic environment—such as policies toward foreign direct investment, competition and regulation—as well as activity, industry, firm, and individual-directed policies—such as R&D incentives and industry-directed financial incentives. Some instruments could, of course, be placed in more than one classification, such as government procurement or tax policy.

These tools may be used to affect competitive conditions, either in individual situations or for groups of industries, in several different ways. Some instruments—e.g., tariffs, many nontariff barriers and exchange-rate policies—raise the prices producers receive. Others, such as industrial policy-directed government procurement or subsidies to benefit consumers, increase the demand for the product (and may or may not raise its price). Still others—e.g., government loans and equity participation at less than market rates of return, direct financial incentives, manpower training programs, and aid to small businesses—reduce costs. Also, various legal requirements, including performance requirements for foreign investors or, in some sectors, price and entry regulations, can influence evaluations and decisions about the economic attractiveness of particular activities. In varying degrees, Canada uses the full range of policies outlined in Figure 4.

Our review in this chapter is limited to what we judge to be programs having major effects on Canada's industrial structure. A complete examination and assessment of all activities is well beyond the scope of this study. This review is also limited to programs and policies that affect resource processing, manufacturing and energy sectors; programs for agriculture, other resource extraction and services are not discussed, and regulation and small business policies are excluded because it is difficult to discern their impacts. (It should be noted that Canadian health, environmental and safety regulations are probably not as costly—and not as strict—as their U.S. counterparts.) Finally, our attention is primarily focused on federal policies and programs. However, it is important to keep in mind that these are often supplemented by provincial initiatives.

Canadian policies are reviewed in the following order:
International Trade Policies
Policies toward Foreign Direct Investment
Energy Policies
Competition Policies
Research and Development Incentives
Financial Assistance and Tax Policies Favoring Manufacturing
Public Enterprises
Procurement
Manpower Policies.

(Energy policies have been included because Canada's efforts in this area will substantially affect the general development environment and national capacities to undertake industrial development initiatives.)

As this review reveals, the Canadian government is using a wide range of industrial policy tools to encourage increased processing and downstream manufacturing of Canada's natural resources—in addition to their exploitation and export—the development of R&D-intense, high technology industries; the generation of sufficient high quality employment opportunities; and regional equity in the distribution of the opportunities and income from economic development.

INTERNATIONAL TRADE POLICIES

Trade policies have always been an essential element of Canadian industrial policy. As a large country with a small population, Canada has historically depended highly on trade and thus has been significantly influenced by international economic events. The level of Canadian protection has played an important role in determining the level of domestic specialization and the degree to which Canadian industries could be integrated with those of other economies. Further, Canada's market centers are geographically dispersed, and in many cases the pull of U.S. markets on them has been stronger than the natural forces for the development of a more integrated domestic economy. Therefore, Canada's international commercial policies have been a principal determinant of the degree of Canadian development along the east-west axis, as opposed to north-south interrelationships with the United States.

Tariff and Nontariff Protection

As previously discussed, Canada entered the 1970s with tariffs that were generally higher than those of its major trading partners. Like that of other industrial countries, the Canadian tariff structure is progressive in nature, in that it provides more protection for highly fabricated manufactures than for primary commodities and less fabricated manufactures. This tends to give rise to higher rates of *effective protection* for manufacturing industries than for primary industries, although the Tokyo Round tariff cuts being phased in over the 1980–87 period should greatly reduce this tendency.

Also as in other industrial countries, nontariff protection in Canada has become more prominent with the gradual reduction of tariffs under the GATT. Estimates published by the Economic Council of Canada indicate that, as of 1970, tariffs provided the manufacturing sector with an average level of protection of about 9.6 percent, while quotas and subsidies added about 3 more percentage points of protection.[1] Other nontariff barriers, such as discriminatory government procurement, undoubtedly increased the protection afforded by these trade distorting practices, but Canada's use of NTBs was probably no greater than that of other industrial countries.

Further, the manner in which the tariff is applied gives more protection to domestic producers than average nominal tariff rates indicate. For example, the Canadian tariff code provides for split rates in some tariff classifications—higher rates are charged for products of a kind made in Canada than for those that are not.[2] The machinery program established in 1968 embodies this approach; the duty on imported machinery is remitted if comparable equipment is not available from domestic producers. Another example is the use of duty remission agreements to increase produc-

---

1   See Economic Council of Canada, *Looking Outward: A New Trade Strategy for Canada* (Ottawa, 1975), Table 2–6, p. 17.

2   This practice also creates uncertainty as to what rates will be charged and hence may discourage imports.

tion and employment in Canada. Several European automobile manufacturers have agreed to produce and/or purchase components in Canada for reduced duties on their imports of assembled vehicles. In other sectors, multinational corporations have agreed to produce one product line in Canada for reduced duties on their imports of other product lines in the same industry.

On a sectoral basis, there is some variation in the levels of protection given Canadian manufactures. Above average protection is provided to many labor-intense sectors likely to be more adversely affected by imports. These include tobacco processing, textiles and apparel, furniture, leather products, and shipbuilding. Rubber products and electrical equipment also receive above average protection.[3]

Therefore, the structure of protection does tend to encourage increased processing and manufacturing but not necessarily in areas in which Canada may have inherent comparative advantages or in ways consistent with Canadian goals of increasing efficiency and specialization within sectors or of encouraging the rapid development of high technology industries. Further, since the Canadian tariff wall is to be substantially reduced over the 1980–87 period because of agreements negotiated at the Tokyo Round, the legacy of this protective structure will undoubtedly make the Canadian adjustment process difficult, perhaps more so than in many other leading industrial nations. In these circumstances, pressures for extensive adjustment assistance and for increased nontariff protection may be significant.

Export Promotion

The other side of commercial policy is export promotion. Canada has an extensive set of programs, including official assistance for export financing and for export market development.

These programs are recent creations compared to tariff policies. For example, the Export Development Corporation (EDC), discussed below, was established in 1970 through a reorganization of the Export Credit Insurance Corporation (1944), whereas the tariff structure is the result of over 100 years of legislation and international negotiations constrained by domestic political realities. The relatively more recent export promotion programs are more supportive of Canada's economic development objectives of promoting higher technology manufacturing and high quality employment opportunities and are also substantial in size, with credit supports and other expenditures equal to about 5 percent of merchandise exports.[4]

Export Financing. The EDC provides loans, loan guarantees and insurance and foreign investment insurance to Canadian firms. These facilities are not designed to subsidize Canadian firms, but rather to make export credit available on terms competitive with those of other countries. However, Canada's economic development objectives are important factors in allocating funds.

Long-term loans and loan guarantees are available to buyers of capital equipment and technical services. The number of Canadian jobs generated, the *quality* of

---

3   Economic Council of Canada, *Looking Outward*, Table 2–6, p. 17.

4   However, like those of the United States, Canada's efforts in this area are quite modest compared to the export promotion programs of many of the other major industrial countries.

Canadian content and the effects on small and medium-size businesses are important considerations in reviewing loan applications.

Virtually all Canadian exporters may insure up to 90 percent of their export transactions against nonpayment arising from political and most commercial risks.[5] In 1981, the EDC provided direct, guaranteed and insured loans totaling $4.3 billion (see Table 7).

Through the Program for Export Market Development, the Canadian government shares the risk of entering new or expanding existing export markets. PEMD contributes up to 50 percent of project costs, which firms repay at the rate of 1 percent of sales for up to three years if exports result. Assistance is available for participation in major capital projects (e.g., airports and power plants), marketing expenditures (e.g., market identification projects, participation in trade fairs and travel for prospective buyers and exporters), and for forming export consortiums. PEMD participation requires:

> . . . a proven need to share the risk of developing or maintaining overseas markets, bidding on capital projects of unusual size or complexity, unusual international competition, or a need to create an export consortium to meet sales opportunities abroad.[6]

Export Marketing. The Department of External Affairs, having taken over some of the responsibilities of Industry, Trade and Commerce, promotes Canadian exports by providing marketing advice through its Trade Commissioner Service, its International Bureaus and several other programs.

The Trade Commissioner Service maintains representatives in over 60 countries who assist Canadian exporters in locating buyers and help make foreign purchasers aware of Canadian products. In addition:

TABLE 7. DIRECT ASSISTANCE TO EXPORTERS IN CANADA, 1981
($ Can. Millions)

	Grants and Contributions	Loans	Guaranteed and Insured Loans	Total
Export Development Corporation		1,508	2,752	4,260
Program for Export Market Development	23			23
Promotional Projects Program				
Total (percent of merchandise exports)				4,283 5.1%

Sources: Export Development Corporation and the Ministry of State for Economic and Regional Development.

---

5 EDC also provides other services such as insuring Canadian firms against the loss of performance bonds caused by the nonperformance of other members of a consortium.

6 Ministry of State for Economic Development, *Assistance to Business in Canada* (Ottawa: Supply and Services Canada, 1979), p. 127.

> The trade commissioner acts as an export market consultant to Canadian exporters in all phases of marketing, including identification of export opportunities, assessment of market competition, introduction to foreign businessmen and government officials, screening and recommending agents, guidance on terms of payment, and assistance with tariff or access problems.[7]

The International Bureaus also provide foreign marketing information, including data on market prospects and market access information — e.g., background concerning tariffs, import regulations and nontariff barriers. The bureaus maintain a special in-depth advisory service on U.S. customs and access requirements and regulations.

Canadian products are promoted abroad by the Promotional Projects Program. PPP sponsors trade fairs and trade missions and gives financial aid to participating firms as well as aid for potential foreign customers to visit Canada. The government intends to merge PEMD and PPP.

Further, the Canadian Commercial Corporation assists firms in selling to foreign governments. In recent years, the CCC has obtained export contracts to 90 different countries, benefiting over 400 firms. Finally, Canadian exports are promoted through tied bilateral aid administered by the Canadian International Development Agency.

POLICIES TOWARD FOREIGN DIRECT INVESTMENT

For reasons apparent in Table 8, Canada's industrial policy must overlap its policy toward foreign-owned firms. The high, although gradually declining, foreign ownership and control of Canada's industry assures that whatever industrial policy Canada adopts will affect the foreign sector. Conversely — and this is the process explored here — any special treatment of foreign-owned firms will significantly affect the impact of an overall industrial policy.

During the mid-1950s, concern arose in Canada over the compatibility of extensive foreign ownership with Canada's basic economic interests. Although the Royal Commission chaired by Walter Gordon was organized in 1957 to cover the full scope of Canada's economic prospects, it is probably best known for raising the foreign ownership issue. After noting the contributions of foreign investment to Canada, the Gordon Report stated:

> The benefits . . . that we have mentioned are very real and tangible. It is more difficult to state in similarly precise terms what the dangers are in the present situation and what conflicts might occur between the interests of Canadians and the interests of the foreign owners of wholly-owned subsidiaries of foreign companies operating in Canada.[8]

The Gordon Report signaled the beginning of a serious effort to establish appropriate ways to deal with foreign investment. Two impulses have animated this quest. A performance impulse has sought to enlarge Canadian control over foreign firms to assure that they operate in ways more beneficial to national economic objectives. Meanwhile, a more nationalist impulse, more vocal but to date of less consequence, has sought to bring these firms under majority Canadian ownership, apparently assuming

---

7   Ibid., p. 32.

8   *Royal Commission on Canada's Economic Prospects, Final Report* (Gordon Report), (Ottawa: Queen's Printer, November 1957), p. 389.

TABLE 8. FOREIGN OWNERSHIP AND CONTROL OF CANADA'S MAJOR NONFINANCIAL INDUSTRIES, 1970 AND 1976[1]
(Percent)

		Foreign Ownership			Foreign Control		
		Total	U.S.	Other	Total	U.S.	Other
Petroleum & natural gas	1970	61	50	11	76	61	15
	1976	51	40	11	68	54	14
Other mining & smelting	1970	59	48	11	70	59	11
	1976	57	45	12	55	41	14
Manufacturing, total	1970	53	45	8	61	47	14
	1976	50	41	9	55	42	13
Beverages	1970	30	24	6	40	n.a.	n.a.
	1976	31	21	10	29	n.a.	n.a.
Rubber	1970	69	n.a.	n.a.	99	n.a.	n.a.
	1976	73	n.a.	n.a.	98	n.a.	n.a.
Textiles	1970	24	17	7	26	19	7
	1976	27	21	6	32	22	10
Pulp & paper	1970	60	49	11	53	38	15
	1976	53	41	12	42	29	13
Agricultural machinery[2]	1970	64	n.a.	n.a.	55	n.a.	n.a.
	1976	52	n.a.	n.a.	50	n.a.	n.a.
Automobiles & parts	1970	87	n.a.	n.a.	97	n.a.	n.a.
	1976	92	n.a.	n.a.	96	n.a.	n.a.
Other transportation equipment	1970	52	37	15	65	43	22
	1976	45	34	11	54	38	16
Iron & steel mills	1970	11	7	4	1	1	0
	1976	11	9	2	2	n.a.	n.a.
Aluminum	1970	76	67	9	100	n.a.	n.a.
	1976	54	42	12	0	0	0
Electrical apparatus	1970	61	55	6	73	63	10
	1976	66	58	8	73	62	11
Chemicals	1970	66	52	14	81	58	23
	1976	66	52	14	74	58	16
Other manufacturing	1970	49	41	8	60	44	16
	1976	49	39	10	62	46	16

n.a. = U.S. data are not presented separately.
[1]"The series on ownership and control show the relative positions of Canadian and foreign investments in Canadian non-financial industries. These estimates provide measures of, on the one hand, the proportions of long-term capital invested by Canadians and by nonresidents in Canadian enterprises and, on the other hand, the proportions of total capital employed in Canadian-controlled and in nonresident-controlled enterprises. The first of these measures is termed 'owner-ship' and the second 'control.' It should be noted that 'foreign ownership' includes portfolio holdings of nonresidents as well as foreign direct investment, while the data on foreign-controlled investment include investment by Canadians and investors from third countries in enterprises controlled by nonresidents." See source below.
[2]Includes establishments engaged in the production of other heavy equipment, which tends to overstate percentages for agricultural machinery only.
Source: Data and explanation in footnote 1 from *Statistics Canada Daily* (November 24, 1980), p. 4 and pp. 6–9.

that this action by itself would contribute significantly to their better performance in terms of national goals.[9]

The gestation of Canadian policy toward foreign ownership since the Gordon Report can be divided into four periods: (1) actions during the mid-1960s; (2) official studies between then and 1972, leading to (3) establishment of the Foreign Investment Review Agency in 1973; and (4) "Canadianization" initiatives that surfaced in 1980.

Policy Actions during the Mid-1960s[10]

The first initiative, and still an important one, was to impose within the *Canada-U.S. Automotive Agreement of 1965* certain conditions on foreign (all U.S.-owned) vehicle firms. The agreement enables these firms to import new vehicles and associated components duty free from the United States, but only if they meet specific requirements for increasing production in Canada.[11] This application of so-called performance requirements was an important milestone in Canadian policy toward foreign investment and signaled a predominance of the performance impulse over the nationalist impulse that has persisted, at least until now. Indeed, the Auto Agreement should be seen as a significant step in foreign investment policy rather than in bilateral trade policy, where it is usually classified.

In the second action during this period, the Canadian government in 1966 circulated to 3,500 active foreign subsidiaries some *Guidelines of Good Corporate Citizenship* (Figure 5). These voluntary principles urged foreign firms to orient their policies affecting a wide range of matters—such as product specialization, exports, domestic procurement, R&D, and Canadian management—to enhance their net contribution to Canadian economic development. As such, these guidelines stand as the first comprehensive statement of performance goals for foreign investment, and thus to some extent as an early articulation of Canadian industrial policy objectives.[12] That this constellation of principles has remained basically the same over the years reveals that by the mid-1960s Canadian officials had developed a fairly settled understanding

---

9   This section does not imply that the United States is not concerned over increasing levels of foreign ownership within the United States. Interest in some of the same issues described here has been mounting, although with less urgency and against the backdrop of a general policy of neutrality toward foreign direct investment. Nevertheless, congressional concern exists as signaled in the Twentieth Report by the U.S. Congress, House Committee on Governmental Operations, *The Adequacy of the Federal Response to Foreign Investment in the United States*, 96th Cong., 2d sess., 1980. The subject is extensively reviewed in "Canadian-American Investment Relations," by Gary C. Haufbauer and Andrew J. Samet (forthcoming).

10   A number of other ad hoc actions were undertaken before the mid-1960s, including the Eisenhower-Diefenbaker Statement in 1958 and the Fulton-Rogers Agreement on antitrust in 1959, as well as various measures to favor ownership by Canadian citizens or to require more complete disclosure of subsidiary activity. These are omitted from this review as being less central to the development of Canadian industrial policy.

11   As discussed in Appendix 1 and noted in Chapter 2, the performance requirements of the Automotive Agreement were anticipated by somewhat similar unilateral conditions in the two duty remission schemes that Canada applied to this industry, which had to be abandoned as likely to trigger countervailing action by the United States.

12   Lesser known, but perhaps as significant because of its origin, is a quite similar list of guidelines entitled "Precepts for Successful Business Operating Procedures in Canada and the United States," developed in 1968 by a Canada-U.S. committee sponsored by the Canadian and U.S. Chambers of Commerce.

FIGURE 5. MEASURES TO INCREASE BENEFITS AND REDUCE COSTS OF FOREIGN DIRECT INVESTMENT*

Guidelines of Good Corporate Citizenship

A further response to growing foreign control was the issuance in 1966 of guiding principles of good corporate behavior for Canadian subsidiaries of foreign firms. These were announced by the then Minister of Trade and Commerce, the Honorable Robert Winters.

The guidelines provide as follows:

(a) pursuit of sound growth and full realization of the company's productive potential, thereby sharing the national objective of full and effective use of the nation's resources;

(b) realization of maximum competitiveness through the most effective use of the company's own resources, recognizing the desirability of progressively *achieving appropriate specialization of productive operations* within the internationally affiliated group of companies;

(c) *maximum development of market opportunities in other countries* as well as in Canada;

(d) where applicable, *to extend processing of natural resource products* to the extent practicable on an economic basis;

(e) pursuit of a pricing policy designed to assure a fair and reasonable return to the company and to Canada for all goods and services sold abroad, including sales to the parent company and other foreign affiliates;

(f) in matters of procurement, *to search out and develop economic sources of supply in Canada;*

(g) to *develop* as an integral part of the *Canadian* operation wherever practicable, the *technological,*

research and design capability necessary to enable the company to pursue appropriate product development programs so as to take full advantage of market opportunities domestically and abroad;

(h) retention of a sufficient share of earnings to give appropriate financial support to the growth requirements of the Canadian operation, having in mind a fair return to shareholders on capital invested;

(i) to work toward a Canadian outlook within management, through purposeful training programs, *promotion of qualified Canadian personnel* and inclusion of a major proportion of Canadian citizens on its board of directors;

(j) to have the objective of a financial structure which provides opportunity for equity participation in the Canadian enterprise by the Canadian public;

(k) periodically to publish information on the financial position and operations of the company; and

(l) to give appropriate attention and support to recognized national objectives and established government programs designed to further Canada's economic development and to encourage and support Canadian institutions directed toward the intellectual, social and cultural advancement of the community.

*Italics added.
Source: Reprinted from *Foreign Direct Investment in Canada* (Gray Report), (Ottawa: Government in Canada, 1972), pp. 324–25.

of how they intended to monitor, and thus presumably influence, the performance of foreign-owned firms. Unlike the Auto Agreement, however, the 1966 guiding principles remained only a statement of aspirations. Experience with them brought out two shortcomings: (1) foreign firms would comply with performance goals only if these were mandatory; and (2) since the guidelines did not also apply to Canadian-controlled firms, "no yardstick exists against which the performance of the foreign-controlled firms may be measured."[13] The first deficiency was subsequently eliminated by administrative intervention in the FIRA process. The second, although frequently mentioned, has never been remedied.

Official Studies, 1968–72

Around 1967–68, Canadian-American relations appeared to shift from a relatively easy postwar period into a more contentious era.[14] One evidence of this was a deter-

---

13   From *Foreign Direct Investment in Canada* (Gray Report), (Ottawa: Government in Canada, 1972), p. 325.

14   This view is discussed in *The New Environment for Canadian-American Relations*, a Statement by the Canadian-American Committee (Washington, D.C., September 1972), pp. 3–4.

mination by the Canadian government to develop and enact a coherent and enforce-
able strategy for dealing with foreign ownership. Accordingly, it set up a succession of
three study groups.

In 1967, Prime Minister Pearson appointed eight leading academic economists to
the *Watkins Task Force*. Its charge was ". . . to analyze the causes and consequences of
foreign investment, to assess actual benefits and costs, and to put forth proposals for
legislative consideration."[15] The Watkins Report, issued in January 1968, deplored the
"piecemeal and gradual" reactions of present Canadian policy to foreign investment
and advocated a single, coherent policy.

> The major deficiency in Canadian policy has been not its liberality toward foreign investment
> *per se* but the absence of an integrated set of policies, partly with respect to both foreign and
> domestic firms, partly with respect only to foreign firms, to ensure higher benefits and smaller
> costs for Canadians from their operations of multi-national corporations.[16]

The mention here of "domestic firms" was a significant early expression of the view
that it was desirable to apply policy prescriptions to all firms — foreign and domestic —
operating in Canada.

A central recommendation of the Watkins Report was the creation of a government agency to coordinate policies with respect to foreign-owned firms, to undertake
surveillance of their operations and to administer the 1966 guidelines, which were to
be made mandatory. Most important in terms of the development of industrial policy
thinking, the report recommended improvement of the environment for *all* industry in
Canada as being indispensable to any effective policy for foreign-owned firms.

> The size of the net economic benefit to Canada from foreign direct investment depends
> critically on whether foreign factors of production are used efficiently in Canada and on
> whether the quality of Canadian factors of production is high so that foreign firms operate in
> an environment of efficient performance by domestic firms. Without an appropriate set of in-
> dustrial policies which create an efficient structure of industry in Canada, the benefits of
> foreign direct investment tend to be emasculated.[17]

As for the goal of greater Canadian participation, the main recommendation
to be implemented was the creation in 1971 of the Canada Development Corporation, a large holding company with entrepreneurial and management functions,
to assume a leadership role in Canada's business and financial community in close
cooperation with existing institutions.[18] (The CDC is discussed later.) Otherwise the
government did not act on the report, which left it to represent only the views of its

---

15   David Godfrey and Mel Watkins, eds., *Gordon to Watkins to You, A Documentary: The Battle for Control of Our
Economy* (Toronto: New Press, 1970), p. 64.

16   *Foreign Ownership and the Structure of Canadian Industry* (Watkins Report), (Ottawa: Queen's Printer, 1968), p. 392.

17   Ibid., p. 404.

18   Ibid., p. 411. The Watkins Report was also responsible for certain innovations not usually associated with it, such as
the improved collection of information undertaken by the Department of Industry and under the Corporation and Labour
Unions Returns Act, and work on imperfections of competition, leading, in part, to the Phase I legislation on combines in
the early 1970s.

authors.[19] But it did lay the foundation for two subsequent study groups that were convened in 1970.

The *Wahn Committee*, a parliamentary standing committee, was created to study Canada-U.S. relations generally, but with considerable emphasis on "American Ownership and Control of Canadian Resources and Industry." Its report (published in late 1970) supported the view that Canadian ownership should be raised to a majority position in all companies operating in Canada. While acknowledging that the capital required to accomplish the "buy back" might be unavailable for many years, and even then "involve a massive misallocation of scarce Canadian capital resources," the report stated:

> Nevertheless, the Committee recognizes that as a general rule it is desirable that Canadians should control Canadian companies by owning at least 51% of their voting shares, particularly in the important sectors of the economy where American control is now most highly concentrated, and that we should move toward this goal as rapidly as capital requirements and other relevant circumstances permit.[20]

Aside from encouraging consideration of the buy-back approach to foreign ownership, the Wahn Report had little impact, in part because the government had simultaneously launched in 1970 what proved to be the definitive study of a cohesive strategy for dealing with foreign-owned firms by the *Gray Task Force*, named for its chairman Herb Gray, the current Minister of Regional Industrial Expansion.

In 1972, this group produced the most comprehensive and influential product of the three official study groups, the 500-page Gray Report, which undertook two tasks. First, it analyzed the impact and implications of the high degree of foreign control of Canadian business. In so doing it introduced the concept of "truncation," which held that certain corporate functions particularly beneficial to Canada, such as R&D activities, tended to be performed abroad by the parent firms. It followed that Canada's foreign investment policy should be oriented largely to neutralizing truncation by interventionist approaches relevant only to foreign-owned firms.

Second, the Gray Report canvassed the range of policy options enabling Canadians to exercise greater control over their national economic endowment, to maximize the net benefits to Canada of foreign direct investment and, where feasible, to retain and increase Canadian ownership of their business activity. Three policy options were examined. The "key sector" approach would reserve certain "commanding heights" of the economy wholly or partially for Canadian ownership and control. The "fixed rules" approach would set minimum levels for mandatory Canadian participation in the ownership and/or direction of all foreign-owned firms. The third approach would call for administrative review of designated categories of foreign investment, screening each case in keeping with performance criteria to be set by legislation.

Rejecting the first two approaches, the Gray Report proposed setting up a screening mechanism, which emerged as the Foreign Investment Review Agency.

---

19   However, the nature and status of the Watkins Report were somewhat obscured by its partial repudiation by Professor Watkins, who had moved to a position advocating nationalization as the ultimate solution to the basic problems of foreign ownership in Canada.

20   *Eleventh Report of the Parliamentary Standing Committee on External Affairs and National Defense*, Special Committee Respecting Canada-U.S. Relations (Wahn Report), (Ottawa: Queen's Printer, 1970), Section 7.07.

The Foreign Investment Review Agency

The establishment of FIRA in 1973 served notice that Canada:

- was de-emphasizing—at least for the time being—the goal of buying back foreign subsidiaries and would concentrate instead on gaining more control over how they operated in Canada;

- was committed to backing up its screening of foreign-owned firms by administrative intervention to assure their performance met certain agreed objectives.

Since April 1974, FIRA has undertaken prior review and approval of foreign acquisitions of Canadian businesses—including their transfer from one foreign owner to another—with gross assets of $250,000 or more or gross revenues of $3 million or more. In October 1975, FIRA extended its operations to cover new businesses established in Canada by foreigners. (As these are the two methods by which foreign subsidiaries expand, the firms that are dynamic will contend, sooner or later, with FIRA's review procedures.) In this process, FIRA advises and assists the Minister of Regional Industrial Expansion, who in turn reports to the Cabinet, which has ultimate responsibility for a particular decision.

FIRA judges foreign investment proposals against their potential to bring "significant benefits to Canada." Ten criteria have emerged by which each proposal is judged. These are ranked in Table 9 by the number of times the 2,685 proposals accepted dur-

TABLE 9. REASONS FOR FIRA ACCEPTANCE OF FOREIGN INVESTMENT PROPOSALS, 1974-75 THROUGH FIRST QUARTER 1981-82[1]
(Total Accepted Proposals: 2,685)

Rank	Criterion for Acceptance	Number of Times Employed[2]	Percent of Total Accepted Proposals
(1)	Compatibility with national industrial and economic policies	2,540	95
(2)	New investment	2,134	79
(3)	Increased employment	2,125	79
(4)	Increased resource processing or use of Canadian products or services	1,635	61
(5)	Canadian participation (as shareholders/directors/managers)	1,575	59
(6)	Improved product variety and innovation	1,141	42
(7)	Improved productivity and industrial efficiency	1,107	41
(8)	Additional exports	987	37
(9)	Beneficial impact on competition	705	26
(10)	Enhanced technological development	555	21

[1]The 33 cases accepted during the first year of operation (1974-75) are not counted since no data are available on the criteria for their acceptance.
[2]Typically, several reasons are given when a proposal is accepted; on rare occasions, all 10 of them may be used.
Sources: 1974-75 through 1976-77: Christopher Green, *Canadian Industrial Organization and Policy* (Toronto: McGraw-Hill Ryerson, 1980), p. 312. 1977-78 through 1980-81: compiled from *Foreign Investment Review Acts Annual Reports* for these years and *Foreign Investment Review Acts Quarterly Report, April to June 1981*.

ing the seven-year period to date fulfilled each test. The top ranking two—compatibility with national industrial and economic policies and new investment—are, respectively, too broad and too automatic to signal any meaningful priority. The highest scoring specific criteria are increasing employment and the sourcing of goods and services within Canada. Meanwhile, the goals of generating additional exports and enhancing technological development, despite the public emphasis they receive, are among the least cited criteria. An interesting question is whether this ranking shows the relative importance assigned these criteria by FIRA or reflects the preferences of foreign investors regarding their plans and the areas in which they are willing to make concessions. What is clear from the nature and frequency with which the criteria have been cited is the importance of FIRA as a vehicle for leveraging foreign private resources to achieve important industrial policy objectives. Through its screening of foreign investment proposals, FIRA has been able to commit parent firms to a wide range of actions benefiting Canada. Figure 6 lists 13 such undertakings by a U.S. computer firm preceding FIRA approval of its application in 1981.

Over the 1974–80 period, FIRA approved about 85 percent of all proposals submitted for its formal review, which some Canadians interpret as being too lenient. In 1979–80, some 92 percent of decided cases were allowed and in 1980–81 almost 88 percent. These figures mask, however, the extent to which proposals were withdrawn or "improved" in terms of FIRA criteria before formal submission.

What is the potential of FIRA? At present, it represents a framework for industrial strategy applied via administrative intervention in the two methods of transferring or expanding foreign investment. This beachhead could possibly be expanded along two axes.

FIGURE 6. PERFORMANCE COMMITMENTS TO FIRA: THE CASE OF A U.S. COMPUTER COMPANY

The Honorable Herb Gray, then Minister of Industry, Trade and Commerce, announced that on September 21, 1981 Apple Inc. of California made the following undertakings prior to receiving FIRA approval of its investment application:

(1) to make all officers, except the Chairman of the Board and the Secretary, and all management resident Canadians;

(2) to limit appointments of nonresidents to one year or less;

(3) to sell at least 80 percent of its product through independent Canadian retailers (unless market conditions require the use of company personnel to make direct sales);

(4) to perform in Canada at least 80 percent of all repair and maintenance service for products manufactured by the applicant or the new business and sold in Canada;

(5) to seek actively and recommend to customers Canadian sources of compatible peripherals and materials subject to availability in sufficient quantities;

(6) to commence manufacturing in Canada, when sales justify establishment of a "module" employing approximately 100 people (anticipated within three years), and to review RPT progress toward this goal with the Department of Industry, Trade and Commerce twice a year;

(7) to implement vigorously an existing agreement providing for the use of telidon interface kits (TIKs) dedicating Apple and its subsidiaries to the creation of a world market for TIKs;

(8) to seek actively and develop Canadian sources for Canadian-made goods if competitively available (specifically power supply units and semi-conductor memories). ("For such purposes, complete information will be provided to Canadian suppliers regarding future worldwide requirements of the applicant, industry prices, and technology which the applicant is not restricted from communicating by previous agreements with third parties and which, in the judgment of the applicant, is required by such suppliers.");

(9) to establish a corporate purchasing task force with the specific mandate of identifying and developing Canadian sources of supply for Apple's worldwide requirements;

(10) to recommend to its worldwide dealers Canadian-made peripheral equipment, provided such products are competitive in price, performance and availability;

(11) to ensure that at the end of the first year Canadian value-added (CVA) will not be less than 38 percent of the cost of goods sold in Canada, and thereafter to make best efforts to achieve the highest level of CVA in accordance with the schedule (not available because of FIRA's secrecy regulations) submitted to FIRA by the applicant;

(12) to establish within one year a Canadian software research and development group; and

(13) to make best efforts to initiate R&D projects related to hardware.

Source: Office of the U.S. Trade Representative.

One path would be to extend the FIRA review to the performance of all major foreign firms operating in Canada, including those that propose no expansion via acquisitions or new investments. Such wider coverage was implied in the first sentence of a paragraph on foreign ownership in the April 1980 Speech from the Throne.

> The Foreign Investment Review Act will be amended to provide for performance reviews of how large foreign firms are meeting the test of bringing substantial benefits to Canada. As well, amendments will be introduced to ensure that major acquisition proposals by foreign companies will be publicized prior to a governmental decision on their acceptability. The Government will assist Canadian companies wishing to repatriate assets or to bid for ownership or control of companies subject to takeover offers by non-Canadians.

The thrust toward buy backs was muted at least temporarily in mid-1981 with an effort by federal monetary authorities to constrain Canadian bank financing both for Canadian purchases of foreign-owned and -controlled firms and for Canadian corporate initiatives to acquire firms owned and controlled in the United States. The proximate reason for this was a large surge in net direct capital outflow from Canada to the United States that tended to depress the Canadian dollar vis-à-vis the U.S. dollar in the exchange markets. This action and the others foreseen in the above paragraph were officially postponed by a statement on ownership of Canadian industry in the November 1981 pronouncement on economic development policy.

> In the Speech from the Throne in the Spring of 1980, reference was made to three specific measures, two of which involved changes to the Foreign Investment Review Act. For the time being, no legislative action is intended on these measures until progress on the major initiatives already undertaken by the government has been assessed.[21]

Another possibility would be to extend FIRA's administrative intervention to domestically owned firms. Prospects here are ambiguous. On the one hand, we have noted support for such a move during the formative period of Canada's foreign investment policy. Further, this extension would avoid the situation in which Canada applies other than "national treatment" to firms owned abroad, an issue of particular concern just now to U.S. policymakers in connection with Canada's National Energy Program. On the other hand, the extension of FIRA's performance requirements to domestic firms would contradict an explicit conclusion of the Gray Report that "there are several reasons for restricting administrative intervention to foreign-controlled firms."[22] In more practical terms, such a move would amount to a radical advance of governmental control over business in Canada and would undoubtedly be met with considerable resistance.

The "Canadianization" Initiatives of 1980

Two announcements in 1980 appeared to indicate a policy shift from exclusively expanding Canadian *control* over foreign-owned firms, via performance requirements, to increasing Canadian *ownership* of them. The second and third sentences of the Throne Speech excerpt promised steps to assist Canadians retain or acquire corporate

---

21   Government of Canada, *Economic Development for Canada in the 1980s* (November 12, 1981), p. 13.

22   Gray Report, pp. 441–442.

assets, although, as just quoted, actions along these lines were at least postponed by the November 1981 statement.

The actual innovation of "Canadianization" appeared, of course, as a central feature of the October 1980 National Energy Program, to be discussed next. By insisting on achieving majority Canadian ownership by 1990, regardless of the performance of the foreign firms in the oil and gas industry, the NEP represents a significant policy departure. The central question has been whether the Canadianization aspect represents a unique action or a beachhead to be expanded. On this point, the November 1981 statement was far more positive than on questions related to FIRA. "The special measures being employed to achieve more Canadian ownership and control of the oil and gas industry are not, in the Government of Canada's view, appropriate for other sectors."[23]

ENERGY POLICIES

The Canadian energy sector probably has endured as much government intervention as that in most industrial countries. Since the 1973 oil embargo, Canada has pursued an energy policy with three basic aims:

- to minimize Canadian dependence on imported oil;
- to insulate somewhat Canadian consumers from increases in world oil prices;
- to reduce foreign control in the ownership and development of Canadian energy resources (as of October 1980, foreign-held corporations were producing over 70 percent of Canadian oil and gas; see Figure 7[24]).

To serve the first objective, Canada has almost completely phased out net exports of crude oil to the United States and extended its petroleum and natural gas pipeline distribution systems further into eastern Canada.

To serve the second, domestic crude oil prices have been regulated, while oil imports have been subsidized by the federal government. (As of 1979, Canada imported 12 percent of its 1.8 million barrels a day oil requirements.[25]) As a consequence, Canadians have enjoyed prices substantially below comparable U.S. prices (see Figure 8).

To extend Canadian ownership, the third aim, Petro-Canada (PetroCan, a federal Crown corporation) was created in 1975, and the Canada Development Corporation has acquired oil and gas properties. The National Energy Program contains tax changes and development incentives intended to encourage greater participation in the oil and gas industry by Canadians.

The National Energy Program

The NEP, unveiled in October 1980, was modified in September 1981 subject to an agreement with Alberta regarding oil and gas prices, taxes and revenue sharing.[26]

---

23   Government of Canada, *Economic Development*, p. 12.

24   Ministry of Energy, Mines and Resources, *The National Energy Program, 1980* (Ottawa, 1980), p. 20.

25   These are net imports. It is important to note that Canadian vulnerability to import disruptions is somewhat greater than net import figures indicate, because some of the crude oil exported cannot be used to replace imports as a result of the specific requirements of Canadian refineries.

26   "Memorandum of Agreement between the Government of Canada and Government of Alberta Relating to Energy Prices and Taxation" (September 1, 1981).

FIGURE 7. THE LARGEST OIL AND GAS PRODUCING COMPANIES IN CANADA, 1979

Rank	Foreign Controlled	Canadian Controlled
1.	Imperial	
2.	Gulf	
3.	Texaco	
4.	Shell	
5.	Amoco	
6.	Mobil	
7.		Petro-Canada
8.	Hudson's Bay Oil & Gas	
9.	Chevron Standard	
10.	Suncor	
11.		Pan Canadian
12.		Dome
13.	Canadian Superior	
14.	Aquitaine	
15.		Norcen
16.		Home
17.	Canada Cities	
18.	Petrofina	
19.		Husky
20.	BP Canada	
21.	Amerada	
22.	Union Oil	
23.	Chevron Canada	
24.		Alberta Energy
25.		Ocelot
Total Sales* by Group	$6,151 million	$1,608 million
Share of All Industry Sales	71.7%	18.7%

*Net revenues after royalties but before operating costs.

Source: Reproduced from Ministry of Energy, Mines and Resources, *The National Energy Program, 1980* (Ottawa, 1980), p. 20.

The program indicates that the present government intends to keep crude oil prices below U.S. levels and, furthermore, that it is determined to pursue a vigorous program of reducing foreign ownership in the energy sector. The goal is to increase Canadian ownership to 50 percent by 1990. In addition, the NEP is assisting the government's industrial development program by freeing and raising substantial new revenues, some of which have been transferred to the economic and regional development envelope.

The government will continue crude oil price regulations but is phasing out government-financed subsidies for oil imports.[27] The program essentially established a two-tiered pricing structure. The price of old oil—oil in production prior to December 31, 1980—will increase from less than 50 percent of world prices in the summer of 1981 to about 75 percent of world prices over a period of several years. New oil will

---

27 Technically speaking, oil import subsidies are not being eliminated—only their costs to the government and benefits to consumers have disappeared. A tax—the Petroleum Compensation Charge—is being imposed on the use of all crude oil purchased by refiners to finance subsidies for the use of imported and synthetic oil, and this is being passed on to consumers.

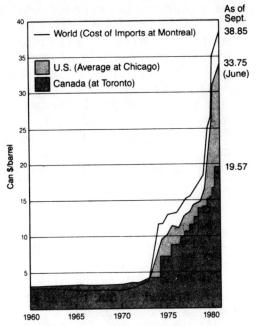

FIGURE 8. CRUDE OIL PRICES: WORLD, UNITED STATES, CANADA, 1960–80

Source: Reproduced from Ministry of Energy, Mines and Resources, *The National Energy Program, 1980* (Ottawa, 1980), p. 4.

likely be priced at or near world market levels. Domestic consumers pay an average of the domestic and import prices, a so-called blended price. Further, the regulated price of natural gas will not increase as quickly as the price of oil to encourage substitution of natural gas for oil. As of July 1981, the price of natural gas was about 75 percent of the price of crude oil on an equivalent Btu basis, with plans to reduce this figure to about 65 percent.

The current government is changing the tax treatment of oil and gas revenues. The NEP provides for modifications in the corporate tax provisions: depletion allowances, which encouraged exploration and development activity and were equally available to foreign and domestic firms, are being phased out. These are being replaced by a complex system of direct incentives that increase with the Canadian ownership of each well. The NEP also imposes taxes on the production of crude oil and natural gas, and a windfall profits tax on old oil revenues, to capture more of their economic rents. Some of these new revenues are being shared by the producing provinces (principally through a Western Development Fund), some are being used as incentives for new energy exploration and development by Canadians, and some are being allocated for general budgetary purposes.

The desired net effect of the increased taxes and the incentives for exploration and development is to make exploration and development on comparable properties more profitable if undertaken by Canadian companies than if undertaken by foreign companies. This encourages foreign firms to enter into more joint ventures with Canadians or to sell their oil and gas assets to Canadians at lower prices than would have been the case had they received the same treatment as Canadian firms.

The NEP supplements these tax and incentive measures with a requirement that the federal government receive a 25 percent buy-in option on all leases on the federally owned Canada Lands, which include virtually all offshore areas, the Yukon and Northwest Territories. (At the time production permits are granted, the federal government may purchase up to 25 percent interest in production operations by bearing up to 25 percent of the development expenses.) Further, the NEP announced that PetroCan would acquire one or more multinational oil companies, with purchases to be financed through additional production taxes. Acting on this mandate, in 1981 PetroCan bought a controlling interest in Petrofina Canada, formerly a Belgian-owned company, and renamed it Petro-Canada Enterprises, Inc. Also, in 1981 the Canada Development Corporation purchased about 75 percent of the Aquitaine Company of Canada from the Société Nationale Elf Aquitaine of France and purchased the remaining outstanding shares.

Impact of the NEP

It is too early to know all the consequences of Canada's NEP, as several important elements were worked out only with the September 1981 agreement between the governments of Canada and Alberta concerning prices and taxation. Here, the program is analyzed on the basis of the data in the NEP and the Ottawa-Edmonton "Memorandum of Agreement." And this program may yet have to be amended in the light of changing conditions in the world oil market.[28]

First, the energy pricing regime will continue to provide a subsidy, and hence international cost advantages, to Canadian producers in industries that directly use large amounts of petroleum and natural gas, such as basic petrochemicals, synthetic textiles and basic plastic products. In the future, Canada may be confronted by countervailing duties in the United States and other industrial countries if this cost advantage is determined to be an export subsidy.

Second, the anticipated federal revenues generated by the new oil and gas tax initiatives and the revenues that are, in effect, freed up by the phased elimination of petroleum import subsidies exceed the government's anticipated expenditures on new energy sector initiatives. In the October 1980 and November 1981 budgets, the federal government indicated that it plans to use some of this revenue gain to increase spending on economic development (industrial policy) and reduce the deficit. But in 1982 the recession is having significant negative effects on revenues and is raising expenditures, increasing the deficit substantially beyond levels anticipated in 1981. The consequences for future discretionary spending are not yet clear. Table 10 shows federal expenditures by envelope and their rates of growth for 1980–81 to 1985–86 as projected in the November 1981 budget.*

From 1980–81 to 1981–82, overall outlays grew an estimated 16.6 percent. (Outlays exclusive of debt service grew by only 11.9 percent, but rising interest rates greatly increased interest payments on existing debt.) At the same time, energy sector expenditures declined by an estimated 26 percent as a result of the implementation of the NEP. In particular, reductions in the net fiscal burdens imposed by the oil import

---

28 On May 31, 1982, Ottawa announced several adjustments to the NEP, which included price adjustments and temporary tax concessions to assist oil and gas producers, but did not change the general thrust of the NEP.

*   Allan J. MacEachen, Minister of Finance, responded to these issues with a new budget on June 28, 1982. For fiscal year 1982–83, he revealed the government's plans to increase further the economic development expenditures, continue new energy sector programs, undertake other new initiatives, raise new revenues, and accept a deficit much larger than anticipated in November 1981 ($19.5 billion or about 25 percent of outlays instead of the anticipated 14 percent).

TABLE 10. CANADIAN FEDERAL EXPENDITURES BY ENVELOPE, 1980-81 TO 1985-86

	1980-81 Actual	1981-82	1982-83	1983-84	1984-85	1985-86
			Projected			
	($ Can. Millions)					
Economic and regional development	5,183	6,767	7,559	8,644	9,576	10,622
Energy[1]	3,624	2,671	3,039	3,602	4,115	4,779
Social affairs	24,633	27,693	30,150	33,795	37,571	41,683
Justice and legal	1,213	1,399	1,541	1,750	1,930	2,133
Services to government	2,732	3,350	3,448	3,676	3,852	4,213
Parliament	130	140	156	174	192	209
Defense	5,058	5,915	7,000	8,000	8,850	9,800
External affairs	1,421	1,728	2,167	2,508	2,819	3,329
Fiscal arrangements	3,908	4,477	4,971	5,610	6,242	6,901
Adjustments[2]	0	− 535	− 496	− 624	− 607	− 644
Total outlays excluding public debt charges	47,902	53,605	59,535	67,135	74,540	83,025
Public debt	10,687	14,695	16,765	18,015	19,360	20,275
Total outlays	58,589	68,300	76,300	85,150	93,900	103,300
	(Percent of Total)					
Economic and regional development	8.8	9.9	9.9	10.2	10.2	10.3
Energy[1]	6.2	3.9	4.0	4.2	4.4	4.6
Social affairs	42.0	40.5	39.5	39.7	40.0	40.4
Justice and legal	2.1	2.0	2.0	2.1	2.1	2.1
Services to government	4.7	4.9	4.5	4.3	4.1	4.1
Parliament	0.2	0.2	0.2	0.2	0.2	0.2
Defense	8.6	8.7	9.2	9.4	9.4	9.5
External affairs	2.4	2.5	2.8	2.9	3.0	3.2
Fiscal arrangements	6.7	6.6	6.5	6.6	6.6	6.6
Adjustments[2]	0	− 0.8	− 0.6	− 0.6	− 0.6	− 0.5
Total outlays excluding public debt charges	81.8	78.5	78.0	78.8	79.4	80.4
Public debt	18.2	21.5	22.0	21.2	20.6	19.6
Total outlays	100.0	100.0	100.0	100.0	100.0	100.0
Addenda: Deficit						
Millions of dollars	12,668	13,340	10,490	9,550	9,980	10,250
Percent of GNP	4.4	4.0	2.8	2.2	2.1	1.9
Percent of outlays	21.6	19.5	13.7	11.2	10.6	9.9

[1]As a result of the implementation of blended oil pricing, net petroleum compensation payments are reduced to zero in 1982-83. This causes a decline in the envelope in 1981-82 and dampens growth in 1982-83.
[2]Includes a central reserve for overruns on statutory programs, a reserve for an estimate of lapse and other adjustments.
Source: Department of Finance, *The Budget in More Detail* (Ottawa, November 12, 1981), Table 1.2, p. 4 and Table 3.2, pp. 16-17.

subsidy permitted the energy envelope's decline from 6.2 percent of the budget in 1980-81 to an estimated 3.9 percent in 1981-82.

Also during this time, expenditures from the economic and regional development envelope rose by about a projected 31 percent. Expansion of programs to assist industry and promote R&D, labor-force adjustment and others caused this envelope to increase from 8.8 percent of overall outlays in 1980-81 to an estimated 9.9 percent in 1981-82.

From 1981-82 to 1985-86, energy sector expenditures are projected to grow much faster than overall outlays, as new initiatives to promote energy production and conservation are more fully implemented. During this period, energy envelope expenditures are to increase by about 79 percent, while overall expenditures will rise by about 51 percent. As a percentage of the budget, energy sector expenditures are projected to grow from 3.9 percent to 4.6 percent, much less than the 6.2 percent in 1980-81. Economic and regional development expenditures are projected to increase from 9.9 percent of the budget to 10.3 percent, and the deficit is projected to decline from about 20 percent of the budget to 10 percent.

Third, Canadian efforts to buy back a substantial share of the oil and gas industry place a considerable strain on capital markets. Unless the required capital is raised by external borrowing, these efforts will crowd out other domestic investments and increase direct capital outflows. Additional external borrowing will increase Canada's already extremely burdensome external interest payments in the long run.

Fourth, the combined impacts of the NEP's price and tax policies will retard the development of Canada's oil and gas resources, impeding Canada's efforts to achieve independence from imported oil.

Fifth, the combined effects of the NEP's price and tax policies and buy-back program may contribute to foreign investor uncertainty about the desirability of investing in Canada's other industries. The NEP's price and tax policies reduce the cash flow of many energy companies. But they also systematically discriminate against foreign (principally U.S.) firms by limiting their access to exploration and development incentives. The combined effects of the NEP and rigorous FIRA reviews have caused some U.S. firms to seek restraints on Canadian investors in the United States and could adversely affect Canada's ability to attract equity investment in the future.

COMPETITION POLICIES

Competition (antitrust) policies play an important role in some countries' industrial policies. In Europe and Japan, for example, mergers have been permitted, and sometimes encouraged, by governments even when these mergers lead to substantial levels of market concentration if they foster the establishment of large, efficient world-scale firms. Such an affirmative role is lacking in U.S. antitrust philosophy and legislation and its enforcement, since a firm's position vis-à-vis other domestic competitors is by far the most important consideration in evaluating mergers, monopolies and oligopolies.

The laws and legal precedents enforcing competition in Canada are not as strict as U.S. antitrust law. In particular, Canada's statutes restricting collusive agreements (agreements among firms establishing prices, market shares and the like) and for regulating mergers and acquisitions to avoid the concentration of market power have not been as rigorously designed and interpreted, nor as vigorously pursued, as comparable U.S. law.[29]

Efforts to control collusive agreements have been limited by the requirement of Section 32 of the Combines Investigation Act (1923, 1935, 1960, 1976) that such arrangements lessen competition "unduly" to be unlawful. Defining unduly has proved to be a considerable challenge for the Canadian judiciary, and this high standard has restricted enforcement. Further, the act treats collusive agreements, and most other practices that might be construed as reducing competition, as criminal and not civil offenses. Therefore, a higher standard of evidence—proof beyond any reasonable doubt—is necessary to obtain convictions than would be required in a civil proceeding. (Exemptions to the requirements of Section 32 were made in 1960 that are

---

29   As discussed in Chapter 7, a new competition policy bill may be introduced by the Canadian government in the near future, focusing on, among other things, collusive agreements, mergers and monopolies, and practices that could operate to reduce competition in Canadian markets.

consistent with other industrial policy initiatives — i.e., cooperation in R&D activity and exporting.)

Similarly, Section 33 of the Combines Investigation Act makes mergers a criminal offense if they lessen competition to the *public detriment*. Coupled with the requirements of criminal procedures, this has severely limited Section 33's effectiveness. Only one (uncontested) merger conviction has ever been obtained.

These various provisions have allowed Canadian firms more freedom of action than U.S. firms in areas of cooperative agreements and mergers, acquisitions and the expansion of operations. However, with respect to mergers, acquisitions and market concentration, it is important to recognize that Canadian competition policy needs (as well as philosophy) are different from those of the United States. U.S. policies toward market concentration focus primarily on preventing its increase by discouraging, and fighting in court, mergers, acquisitions and market share expansion. Some attention has also been devoted to breaking up or limiting activities of firms with significant market power. U.S. enforcement pays little attention to the competition imposed by foreign producers. Given Canada's small market, such a policy might prove counterproductive because it could impose a significant barrier to the establishment of efficient world-scale firms, or firms with an adequate basis for product-line specialization. Further, to the extent that Canada allows the Tokyo Round tariff reductions to truly open its industrial markets to foreign competition, this competition should impose an increased degree of market discipline on Canadian firms.

It is worth noting again that mergers and acquisitions involving any foreign investor are reviewed by FIRA, whose activities have encompassed a substantial proportion of all mergers and acquisitions that have been taking place in Canada in recent years.

RESEARCH AND DEVELOPMENT INCENTIVES

In 1977, Canada devoted about 1 percent of GDP to R&D and ranked low among the industrial countries in both overall and industrial R&D (see Table 11). This has given rise to concerns about the adequacy of Canadian efforts.

Improving Canada's R&D performance, especially its industrial R&D, and its capacity to produce and export technologically sophisticated products is a vital element in Canada's industrial incentive program. Canada has several important programs in place that subsidize and encourage industrial R&D activity, including special tax deductions and credits, grants and loan programs. Estimates of the assistance provided by these programs are listed in Table 12. In 1980–81, total assistance was conservative-

TABLE 11. R&D SPENDING BY PRINCIPAL FUNDING SECTOR AS A PERCENT OF GDP, 1977

	Government	University	Industry	Other	Total
Canada	0.43	0.13	0.34	0.04	0.92
U.S.	1.22	0.07	1.05	0.05	2.39
France*	0.67	0.10	0.74	0.28	1.79
Germany	0.83		1.11	0.06	2.00
Japan	0.27	0.19	1.12	0.12	1.70

*Includes some or all social science research.
Source: Ministry of State for Science and Technology.

TABLE 12. CANADIAN RESEARCH AND DEVELOPMENT INCENTIVES,
1980–81 ESTIMATES
($ Can. Millions)

	Tax Expenditures	Grants	Loans	Total
First-year tax write-off of capital expenditures	97			97
Investment tax credits	45			45
Industrial Research Assistance Program		25		25
New Technology Employment Program		7		7
Defense Industry Productivity Program		58	16	74
Industrial Energy R&D Program		2		2
Others (minimum)		68		68
Total				316

Sources: Ministry of State for Economic Development, *Assistance to Business in Canada* (Ottawa: Supply and Services Canada, 1981); Department of Finance, *Government of Canada Tax Expenditures Account* (Ottawa, 1980); and Ministry of State for Economic and Regional Development.

ly estimated at over $300 million, which financed at least 20 percent of Canada's industrial R&D expenditures.[30]

Some of these incentives include the deduction of 100 percent of firms' capital and current expenditures for R&D in the year incurred plus 50 percent for expenditures over and above average expenditures for the three previous years. A 10 percent investment credit may also be taken for current and capital expenditures, with additional credits of 10 percent for expenditures undertaken in the Atlantic provinces and the Gaspé and further credits for small businesses. In 1980–81, these two provisions generated tax subsidies estimated to be as large as $142 million.

Canada also encourages firms to undertake applied research through the *Industrial Research Assistance Program*. This program assists firms whose end products have commercial potential. IRAP grants are applied toward professional and technical salaries and were estimated to be $25 million in 1980–81.

The *New Technology Employment Program* helps firms undertake R&D by providing employment subsidies to hire recently graduated scientists, engineers and technicians unable to find work in their fields. This program replaced the Scientific and Technical Employment Program. Estimated expenditures were $7 million in 1980–81.

Defense industry firms may receive assistance through the *Defense Industry Productivity Program*. In 1980–81, DIPP made grants totaling $58 million and loans of $16 million. Also, firms may obtain assistance for R&D activities focused on industrial energy conservation through the *Industrial Energy R&D Program*. IERD grants were estimated to be $2 million in 1980–81.

These programs are supplemented by a variety of others, including financial assistance to encourage commercial applications of government and university research

---

30   In 1979, R&D performed by industry was $1,105 million or 0.4 percent of GNP. Employing this percentage, industry R&D in 1980 was estimated to be $1,224 million. Total assistance of $316 million is 25 percent of $1,224 million.

findings and development of new energy technologies. The latter stress, among other things, the substitution of oil with natural gas and coal and energy-conserving technologies.

In its November 1981 statement on economic development, the current government announced plans to draw together the various R&D incentive programs under a new *Industrial Opportunities Program*. A board of senior officials from the relevant agencies reports to the Minister of Regional Industrial Expansion. "Through the IOP, the federal government's resources to support innovation and development will be carefully targeted to the most promising areas of Canadian industrial strength and excellence."[31]

FINANCIAL ASSISTANCE AND TAX POLICIES FAVORING MANUFACTURING

In addition to the advantages provided through R&D incentives, Canadian manufacturing industries[32] benefit from federal programs designed to encourage structural adjustments toward modernization, to assist firms undertaking risky and innovative ventures, and to encourage investment in economically depressed regions. Table 13 summarizes the most important of these benefits. They include general tax provisions that aid most, if not all, manufacturing industries, the somewhat more specialized assistance provided by the Federal Business Development Bank and other incentive programs, and special programs for selected manufacturing industries.

Tax Incentives

Like all corporate income taxes, the Canadian tax is a complex maze with many special provisions, and a full assessment of its effects on the activities and structure of Canadian business is far beyond the scope of this study. As just discussed, some aspects of the tax structure provide special incentives to R&D activities in processing and manufacturing industries. Attention is focused here on the other provisions that encourage these sectors.

The basic federal corporate tax rate is 46 percent with 10 percent rebated to the provinces. However:

- corporations pay a special 40 percent rate on income derived from manufacturing and processing, which created an estimated tax savings of $600 million in 1980;

- machinery and equipment used in processing and manufacturing may be written off in two years, which provided an estimated tax savings of $500 million in 1980;

- an investment tax credit of 7 percent (10 percent in the Atlantic region and 20 percent in the Gaspé region) is provided for qualified purchases of

---

31   Government of Canada, *Economic Development*, p. 16.

32   Manufacturing is defined here to include resource processing and manufacturing.

TABLE 13. CANADIAN INCENTIVE PROGRAMS AVAILABLE TO MANUFACTURING, 1980-81 ESTIMATES ($ Can. Millions)

	Tax Expenditures	Grants	Direct and Guaranteed Loans	Total
Tax expenditures				
Manufacturing tax incentive	600			600
Machinery deduction	500			500
Investment tax credit	170			170
General incentive programs				
Federal Business Development Bank			886	886
Enterprise Development Program		55	1005	1060
Regional Development Incentives Program		118		118
Small Business Loans Program			408	408
Shipbuilding		83		83
Footwear, clothing and textiles		4		4[1]
Aerospace and defense		58	14	72[2]

[1]Excludes assistance from EDP.
[2]Defense Industry Productivity Program.
Sources: Ministry of State for Economic Development, *Assistance to Business in Canada* (Ottawa: Supply and Services Canada, 1981); Department of Finance, *Government of Canada Tax Expenditures Account* (Ottawa, 1980); Ministry of State for Economic and Regional Development; and Department of Regional Industrial Expansion.

machinery, equipment and buildings for manufacturing and processing; production of minerals, oil and gas; logging; farming; fishing; and the storage of grain. In manufacturing alone, this provision created an estimated tax savings of $170 million in 1980.

General Incentive Programs

Several Canadian government programs provide firms with financing assistance. These are generally designed to help firms adversely affected by trade—e.g., footwear, shipbuilding—and undertaking high risk innovative activities. Programs for the latter generally allocate incentives to small innovative firms in the more technically advanced manufacturing industries.

The *Federal Business Development Bank*, formerly the Industrial Development Bank, is a Crown corporation that supplies capital and technical assistance to enterprises that lack alternative sources of capital at reasonable rates. The FBDB's services are available to virtually any type of business—manufacturing and nonmanufacturing. To be eligible, a firm must provide (or obtain) capital from sources other than the FBDB in an amount sufficient to ensure a continuing interest in the venture's success, and the firm must demonstrate a reasonable expectation of the venture's success. FBDB makes available technical services (e.g., management counseling and training) and loans, loan guarantees, equity financing, leasing, or any combination of these to eligible firms. In 1980–81, the average loan was about $52,000, and the FBDB loaned or guaranteed loans close to $900 million.

The overall objective of the *Enterprise Development Program*, established in 1977, is to enhance the growth of Canadian processing and manufacturing by helping firms become more internationally competitive.

> Recognizing the importance of exports to the growth of the economy and employment, manufacturing and processing firms are generally eligible for all aspects of the Enterprise Development Program. Firms in the service sector are not eligible for loan guarantees unless the proposed project will provide direct, tangible and significant benefit to firms engaged in manufacturing or processing.[33]

This program, like the FBDB, focuses on the needs of small and medium-size businesses taking on high risk or structural adjustment investments that will ultimately lead to an attractive rate of return. The EDP absorbed or replaced a variety of assistance programs, including the Automotive Adjustment Assistance Program, the General Adjustment Assistance Program, the Footwear Tanning and Adjustment Program, the Program for the Advancement of Industrial Technology, the Industrial Design Assistance Program, and the Pharmaceutical Industry Development Program.

In assessing a firm's application, the EDP takes a corporate planner or merchant banker approach and examines the firm's human, financial, physical, and technological resources, its marketing prospects and its plans to exploit market opportunities. The EDP tries to locate alternative private or public financing and provides assistance only if such funds are not obtainable. Assistance is provided through grants (shared-cost projects) and loan guarantees and is available for market studies, productivity improvement studies, industrial design and productive development projects, plant modernization and expansion investments, working capital, and mergers and acquisitions.

According to *Doing Business in Canada*, EDP projects usually include one of the following elements:

- proposal preparation
  - shared costs for the development of relatively complex proposals that are expected to lead to a substantial Enterprise Development Program project;
  - shared costs for market studies that are part of or are expected to lead to a substantial Enterprise Development Program project;
- shared cost projects
  - productivity improvement studies;
  - innovation projects for new or improved products or processes; and
  - industrial design;
- term loan insurance for adjustment projects
  - modernization or expansion of production systems including acquisition of plant and equipment;
  - working capital;
  - mergers and acquisitions.[34]

---

33   Ministry of Industry, Trade and Commerce, *Doing Business in Canada: Federal Incentives to Industry* (Ottawa, 1979), p. H–9.

34   Ibid., p. H–8.

EDP provides up to 50 percent of eligible costs in shared-cost projects and up to 90 percent of costs through guaranteed (insured) loans. In 1980–81, EDP grants were $55 million; loans and loan guarantees totaled slightly more than $1 billion.

Through the *Regional Development Incentives Program* (RDIP, administered by the Department of Regional Industrial Expansion and formerly by DREE), the Canadian government supplies direct incentives grants to firms locating or expanding facilities in specified development regions. Eligibility is generally limited to manufacturing.

> Most manufacturing and processing industries are eligible for development incentives and loan guarantees.
> The major exceptions are petroleum refining, certain parts of the pulp and paper industry, mining, and the growing, harvesting or extracting of natural products. However, the processing of natural products in such operations as sawmills, fertilizer plants, fish plants or other food processing establishments qualifies under the program.[35]

In 1980–81, grants were $118 million. (Canada's principal regional development programs, and their histories, are summarized in Appendix 2.)

General assistance is also provided to industry through the *Small Business Loans Program*, as well as a variety of special technical services, such as management assistance. In 1980–81, these guaranteed loans were $408 million.

Further, over the 1981–84 period, the federal government is supplementing these general programs and its manpower development and assistance programs with a $350 million special *Industry and Labor Adjustment Program*. These funds assist firms and workers in responding to serious industrial dislocations resulting from recent changes in market conditions. The program primarily focuses on selected communities adversely affected by recent plant closures. Firms are encouraged to build facilities in these communities through grants for the costs of consultants for planning and project development and through interest free loans for a portion of eligible capital costs.

Industry-Specific Programs

In addition to general incentive programs, the Canadian government has established various programs to assist specific industries that have encountered particularly strong international competition. In manufacturing, special programs are in place in three sectors: shipbuilding; footwear, clothing and textiles; and aerospace and defense. For example, as mentioned earlier, DIPP assists the defense industry, allocating grants and loans of about $72 million in 1980–81. The benefits provided firms in 1980–81 through these programs are listed in Table 14 (having been summarized earlier in Table 13).

In addition, the *Automotive Adjustment Assistance Program* facilitated structural change during the years following the implementation of the Auto Agreement (1965). As noted, AAAP was subsumed into the activities of EDP in 1977. More recently, the Canadian government provided the Ford Motor Company with a $40 million subsidy to build an engine plant in Windsor, Ontario.

Finally, as discussed in Chapter 7, the federal government announced in June 1981 the establishment of the *Canadian Industrial Renewal Board* to coordinate its efforts to assist the textile and apparel industry.

---

35   Ibid., p. H–5.

**TABLE 14. INDUSTRY-SPECIFIC INCENTIVE PROGRAMS
IN MANUFACTURING, 1980–81 ESTIMATES
($ Can. Millions)**

Program or Service	Purpose and Description	Form of Assistance	
Shipbuilding Assistance			
Shipbuilding Industry Assistance Program (SIAP)	Financial assistance with ship construction.	20% subsidy of building costs.	75
Fishing Vessel Construction Assistance Program	Financial assistance with vessel construction.	Constribution to construction costs.	8
Accelerated capital cost allowances	Rapid write-off.	33 1/3% straight line write-off.	n.a.
Footwear, Clothing and Textiles			
Fashion Design Assistance Program	Fosters Canadian fashion design.	Training in industry, internships.	0.2
Adjustment Assistance Benefits Program	Income support for workers on lay-off.	Support payments to workers.	3.3*
Aerospace and Defense			
Defense Industry Productivity Program (DIPP)	Supports R&D pre-production expenses.	Grants of up to 50% of costs. Loans.	57.9 13.6
Laboratory testing of space components	Supports R&D.	David Florida laboratory provides testing facilities.	n.a.

*1979–80 data.
Source: Ministry of State for Economic Development, *Assistance to Business in Canada* (Ottawa: Supply and Services Canada, 1979 and 1981); and Ministry of State for Economic Development.

PUBLIC ENTERPRISES

In addition to tax incentives and various forms of financial assistance, a government may pursue its industrial policy objectives through direct ownership and management of the means of production. However, such public equity investment may be undertaken for a variety of purposes and becomes an element of industrial policy only when it is undertaken to establish, maintain or accelerate the growth of a particular industry and/or support the incomes of particular labor-force groups or regions. Under such circumstances, public equity is used for activities that would not be attempted by the private sector because the expected rate of return[36] is too low *or* the size of the investment or level of risk[37] is too large. In the former case, the public enterprise receives an implicit subsidy because it is permitted to operate at a below-market rate of return. These activities may require not only initial but continuing infusions of public funds or

---

36   An expected value in a probabilistic sense.

37   Variance of the expected rate of return.

various implicit subsidies if market prospects for the enterprise's operations do not improve. Theoretically, public investments made because projects are too large or entail too much risk for private capital markets yet have adequate expected rates of return are not receiving a public subsidy. If the government or public holding company makes enough high risk investments with adequate expected rates of return, profits and losses should average out. A public investment corporation capitalized through government-guaranteed issues in private capital markets or capitalized in part with public funds to reduce risk can provide a useful and inexpensive vehicle for industrial policy initiatives in high risk/high growth potential industries.

Another reason for public equity investment may be economic nationalism, including policies to buy back control of foreign-owned firms and industries or to capture economic rents resulting from a change in relative prices. Recent initiatives to buy out foreign-owned and -controlled oil and gas companies in Canada are motivated by these objectives. Also, public ownership may be pursued as a substitute for price and entry regulations where natural monopolies are present.[38]

Public ownership is considerably more extensive in Canada than in the United States. In 1973, federal and provincial enterprises employed about 2.8 percent of the Canadian labor force,[39] while the comparable figure for the United States was probably less than half as large.[40] Public ownership is more pervasive in Canada for several reasons.

In Canada, public ownership has often been selected over public regulation of private firms in the utilities and services sectors, where natural monopolies have existed, at least until recently. Public corporations—the so-called Crown corporations— handle many of the basic services that constitute important components of infrastructure and that are provided by regulated private firms in the United States.

Electric power is supplied by provincially owned utilities in eight provinces and telephone service in three provinces. Overseas telecommunications are provided by a federally owned firm, Teleglobe Canada, and domestic interprovincial telecommunications by joint federal/private ventures, Telesat Canada and CN/CP Telecommunications. Also, public ownership has been selected in some service sectors where only limited competition is possible and public regulation would be needed because of the limited size of these Canadian markets. The federal and provincial governments own air, rail, highway, and water transportation companies, although the transportation sector is far from being completely government owned. The federal government also owns the Canadian Broadcasting Company, one of the major radio and television networks.

The federal and provincial governments have established public enterprises or purchased private firms in the mining and manufacturing sectors as well. Green has surveyed this involvement at both governmental levels and finds that public ownership in the mining and manufacturing sectors is not large but has been growing recently. In this area, five industries are particularly prominent—steel, pulp and paper, potash min-

---

38   Much of the factual material presented in the balance of this section was obtained from Christopher Green, *Canadian Industrial Organization and Policy* (Toronto: McGraw-Hill Ryerson, Ltd., 1980), Chapter 9, pp. 249–280 and pp. 304–307.

39   Ibid., p. 253.

40   According to Table 6–8 of the National Income and Product Accounts (*Survey of Current Business*, July 1979), public enterprises employed about 1 percent of the U.S. labor force.

ing, petroleum and natural gas, and aircraft. The motivations behind government involvement here have been somewhat different than its motivations in the service industries, discussed above, which provide the necessary infrastructure for the whole range of agricultural, industrial and service activities.

Two wholly provincially owned public steel firms are Sydney Steel (Nova Scotia) and Sidbec (Quebec). Both facilities were previously owned by the Dominion Steel Company and were purchased to maintain employment and, in Sidbec's case, to help ensure Quebec a position in the steel industry. Both facilities have required substantial subsidies. As part of its industrial policy, Quebec is attempting to create a fully integrated and profitable steel complex out of Sidbec, but this organization has not been able to compete effectively with Canada's major steel producers, which include some of the most efficient in the world.

Canada's provinces have also entered the pulp and paper industry to foster economic development in Newfoundland, Manitoba and Saskatchewan, and to maintain employment in Newfoundland and British Columbia.

In the wake of the events in the world oil market since 1973, Canadian federal and provincial governments have established Crown corporations to undertake direct investments and joint ventures to:

- accelerate the exploration, development and production of hydrocarbons and hydroelectric power to ensure more secure supplies of energy;

- extend Canadian ownership and managerial control in the oil and gas industry;

- ensure that the economic rents accruing to hydrocarbon production as a result of the rising world price of crude oil accrue to Canadians rather than to the foreign producers who control much of the Canadian oil and gas industry.

For example, the federal Crown corporation PetroCan has aggressively undertaken a variety of joint ventures to accelerate the development of conventional oil and gas and synthetic hydrocarbons and, as noted earlier, has purchased controlling interest in Petrofina. Also significant, public corporations have been established by Newfoundland (Churchill Falls Corporation, 1974) and Quebec (SOQUIP, 1969) to develop the northeast's extensive hydroelectric capacity. Ontario (Ontario Energy Corporation, 1974); Saskatchewan (SASKOIL, 1973); Alberta (Alberta Energy Company, a joint venture, 1973)[41]; and British Columbia (B.C. Petroleum Corporation, 1973) have set up corporations to accelerate oil and gas development.

Through this involvement in steel, pulp and paper, petroleum and natural gas, and other sectors, the Canadian federal and provincial governments have exhibited their willingness to undertake direct investments—previously left to private initiative—to achieve a variety of industrial policy goals. Among the motivations behind this involvement are maintaining employment and accelerating the development of critical sectors. However, in some cases the reasons are undoubtedly rooted in economic nationalism. Further, similar motives have influenced the federal and some provincial governments to establish holding companies to extend public equity investment in various sectors.

---

41   The Alberta Energy Corporation is 50 percent owned by the province of Alberta and 50 percent owned by private investors.

As mentioned previously in this chapter, the Canada Development Corporation was formed in 1971 in part out of concern over the extent of foreign ownership in the Canadian economy. The CDC was organized to encourage the development and maintenance of Canadian-owned and -managed corporations through equity investments. It was hoped initially that 90 percent of CDC's equity would be purchased by the public; at the end of 1981, however, the public held 51 percent of the voting stock.[42]

In making investments, CDC seeks effective control of firms with the potential to contribute to national economic development in a way that is consistent with Canadian industrial policy aspirations.

> Industries characterized by large, longer-range development projects, an upgrading of Canadian resources, a high-technological base, and a good potential for building a Canadian presence in international markets are considered.[43]

CDC has invested in petrochemicals, mining, oil and gas, health care industries, electronics, fishing, venture capital, and industrial automation. Through these activities, CDC has supported the Canadian policy of increasing domestic control over natural resources and the industrial policy objective of encouraging accelerated development of resource processing and high technology industry in Canada.

CDC has become an especially important source of venture capital. Its holding company, CDC Ventures, Inc., manages the largest pool of venture capital in Canada and, as of December 31, 1981, had invested in 25 small and medium-size firms.[44] See Table 15 for CDC's investments.

During 1981, CDC announced several new acquisitions and initiatives, which support the national objectives of extending domestic control over Canada's natural resources and achieving an enlarged presence in high technology industries. Among these, CDC acquired 74.8 percent of the Aquitaine Company of Canada from the Société Nationale Elf Acquitaine, a French public corporation, at a cost of $1.2 billion, and acquired the remaining outstanding stock for $400 million. Further, it exchanged its 35 percent interest in Texasgulf plus about $500 million for Texasgulf's Canadian properties. CDC formed Canterra Energy Ltd. by combining the Aquitaine Company, CDC Oil and Gas, and oil, gas and sulfur interests acquired from Texasgulf. Kidd Creek Mines Ltd. was established with the remaining Canadian Texasgulf assets. CDC also entered the industrial automation field with the purchase of 85 percent of Sentrol Systems Ltd. Finally, CDC pursued new initiatives in the electronics and biotechnology fields.

PROCUREMENT

In addition to direct incentives, below-market access to credit, tax expenditures, and direct public ownership, Canada uses procurement to pursue industrial policy goals.

---

42   The government of Canada owns 87.7 percent of the common shares outstanding but carries only 48.5 percent of the vote at shareholder meetings; Canada Development Corporation, *1981 Annual Report.*

43   *Canada Yearbook 1978–79* (Ottawa: Statistics Canada, 1978), p. 883.

44   CDC, *1981 Annual Report.*

TABLE 15. CANADA DEVELOPMENT CORPORATION INVESTMENTS, 1981
     ($ Can. Millions)

Company	Percent Interest	Assets	Activity
Petrosar Ltd.	60	$ 956.4	Primary petrochemicals, diesel and residual fuel oil
Polysar Ltd.	100	1,402.2	Synthetic rubber, latex, chemical and plastic products
Kidd Creek Mines Ltd.	100	1,650.6	Diversified mining and processing (zinc, copper, silver, lead, tin and cadmium concentrates and metals; potash)
Canterra Energy Ltd.	100	2,639.0	Oil and gas exploration and development; sulfur
CDC Life Sciences, Inc.	100	148.3	Pharmaceuticals, biologicals, life sciences contract research services and biotechnology
CDC Data Systems Ltd.	100	236.2	A holding company with majority (at least 50 percent) interest in firms producing word processing equipment, high speed printers, and photocopying and equipment
Fishery Products Ltd.	41	155.9	Harvesting and processing fish products
CDC Ventures, Inc.	100	29.0	Venture capital holding company providing equity financing for small and medium-size businesses at the conceptual or development stage; also participates in ventures with CanWest Corporation, an expansion capital organization
Sentrol Systems Ltd.	85	29.3	Industrial automation equipment, i.e., computer-based control systems

Source: Canada Development Corporation, *1981 Annual Report.*

Prior to the GATT Agreement on Government Procurement, the federal government discriminated against foreign suppliers through explicit, as well as implicit, means. The former included tender lists that discriminated against foreign firms, a 10 percent premium on the Canadian content of manufactured goods, and other requirements encouraging the use of Canadian labor and materials. These practices applied to the purchases of federal departments and agencies and some Crown corporations.

During 1980, the federal government took steps to open up tender lists to foreign firms and eliminate other discriminatory practices for purchases by those federal agencies covered by the new GATT agreement. However, the reforms only apply to purchases of entities explicitly listed in the agreement, which does not include those of the Departments of Transport, Communications, Defense, and many Crown corporations.

Also during 1980, the government restated its objectives for government procurement when it established a *Procurement Review Mechanism* for purchases of goods and services over $2 million and for construction over $10 million (or any other purchases judged to have socioeconomic value). These objectives are set out rather explicitly in Chapter 305 of the Treasury Board's *Administrative Policy Manual*, which establishes the review mechanism.

> The objective of the Procurement Review Mechanism is to obtain lasting benefits from the federal procurement activity beyond the immediate impact of the procurement expenditure itself, toward the economic or social development of Canada.

Sub-objectives are:
- to concentrate initially on *industrial benefits*, particularly in the electronic and other *high technology sectors*;
- to foster those initiatives that would be competitive in world markets or in the domestic market with normal levels of protection;
- to stimulate new product innovation and improvements in production technology;
- to provide improved opportunity for subcontracting to Canadian suppliers, particularly small businesses and suppliers in regions of high unemployment.[45]

The subobjectives clearly state the Canadian government's desire to foster the growth of the industrial sector, particularly high technology activities and innovation, and to promote regionally balanced growth. Further, the Canadian government is willing to pay some additional costs when the benefits to be obtained can be justified. This is explicit in the criteria for deciding whether a purchase should be used to achieve specific economic benefits:

- [when] the value of the procurement will be in excess of $2 million for goods and services, $10 million for construction projects, or (where the socioeconomic impact is judged to be significant) of any value;
- [when] the procurement action is consistent with Canada's obligations under international agreements such as the GATT Agreement on Government Procurement or the Defense Production Sharing Arrangement with the United States;
- [when] the procurement will not be used as a subsidy to support an otherwise unprofitable activity;
- when there are extra costs involved in order to achieve a specific benefit it must be demonstrated that —
  - the activity generated by the procurement has a clear prospect of becoming commercially viable;
  - the socioeconomic benefits are sufficient to justify the extra cost of the procurement; and either
  - the socioeconomic benefits would not be forthcoming in the absence of government assistance; or
  - the procurement will contribute to the exploitation of a strategic opportunity.[46]

Given the limited resources of the present government, it is not surprising that procurement has been identified as a means for achieving industrial policy objectives. It provides a vehicle for the use of money that would be spent in any case to encourage industrial expansion, especially in the technologically advanced sectors. The only immediate financial cost *to the government* is the additional expenditures of choosing contractors who may not offer the best price.[47]

Further, federal procurement policy is being supplemented by other practices that already discriminate or potentially discriminate against U.S. producers but are not covered by the Procurement Code. First, many provinces have adopted buy provincial and/or buy national policies (see Chapter 6). Second, domestic sourcing is a consideration in FIRA reviews and, as such, is one of several criteria for rationing foreign access to Canadian resources and market opportunities. Third, the federal government, as part of the National Energy Program, is seeking to ensure that Canadian manufactur-

---

45   Treasury Board of Canada, *Administrative Policy Manual*, Chapter 305, "Procurement Review," Section 2.1 (italics added).

46   Ibid., Section 2.2.

47   Of course, there may be other dynamic efficiency costs resulting, over time, in lost real GNP.

ers' consultants, contractors and service companies have full opportunity to participate competitively in the supply of goods and services. The Committee on Megaproject Industrial and Regional Benefits (C-MIRB) was established in 1981 to review
procurement for energy mega projects on Canada Lands. This committee replaces the
Advisory Committee on Industrial Benefits, which administered a more limited program. C-MIRB receives analytical and administrative support from the Office of Industrial and Regional Benefits in the Department of Regional Industrial Expansion.

The C-MIRB program is intended to help the government achieve the following
benefits from mega projects:

- increased economic sourcing of equipment and services in Canada emphasizing those with
a substantial level of technological and innovative input by Canadians and value added in
Canada;
- diversification and strengthening of the industrial base of Canada's regions;
- creation of new industrial opportunities in slower growing regions;
- growth and establishment of firms in Canada with autonomous, continuing and competitive capabilities to service domestic and world markets;
- maximum participation and development of Canadian labour and management in all
levels of operations in major projects in Canada;
- increased participation in major projects by firms beneficially owned and controlled by
Canadians;
- exploitation of industrial development opportunities generated by major projects to
enhance research and development;
- increased world product mandates for foreign-owned manufacturing and service companies operating in Canada;
- increased procurement by/for owner/sponsors of Canadian produced goods and services
for their world operations on an internationally competitive basis; and
- increased participation by capable small and medium scale enterprises in the exploitation
of industrial benefits, through, for example, increased sub-contracting.[48]

Clearly, the government would like to use the C-MIRB program to increase industrial
R&D, expand markets for Canadian high technology products, accelerate export
development, and achieve regional development objectives.

Under the C-MIRB program, owners and sponsors of major projects are asked to:

- provide details of their manpower and procurement policies, principles and plans for
review with the C-MIRB in advance of entering contractual arrangements with suppliers of
goods and services;
- consult with the C-MIRB cooperatively to identify capable, competitive Canadian suppliers
of goods and services to bid for major project contracts;
- ensure that pertinent information on planned procurements of goods and services is made
available to prospective Canadian suppliers, including those in regions of economic disparity,
on a timely basis;
- ensure that competitive Canadian firms including small and medium scale enterprises are
included on bidders lists and are accorded a fair and equal opportunity to participate in bidding for contracts involving the supply of goods and services;
- provide a satisfactory debriefing on the quality of respective bids particularly to Canadian
firms, in instances where they fail to compete successfully in order to improve their future
prospects; and

---

48   Press release by the Honorable Herb Gray, Minister of Industry, Trade and Commerce (Ottawa, August 27, 1981). Note
that C-MIRB was referred to in the press release as the Committee on Industrial and Regional Benefits; the name was
subsequently changed. The quoted material has been changed to reflect the new name.

- submit selective or annual reports to the C-MIRB, where necessary, to demonstrate their compliance with the government's industrial benefits objectives and corporate procurement and employment guidelines.[49]

Further, owners and sponsors of major projects are asked to adopt and demonstrate the following policies and practices in their corporate behavior:

- purchasing will be conducted in such a manner that goods and services are obtained on a fair and competitive basis consistent with price, reliability, service and delivery;
- corporate purchasing policy is developed and implemented on the basis of independent authority in decision making in the Canadian operation consistent with achievement of the government's industrial benefits objectives.[50]

According to Canadian policy, C-MIRB's activities are not intended to give Canadian firms an advantage over foreign firms, but just an equal chance to sell goods and services to energy mega project developers.

MANPOWER POLICIES

As has been discussed, the Canadian government offers a variety of aids to firms to modernize, renovate and construct new facilities to adjust to change. The main sources of adjustment assistance for firms are the FBDB, for higher risk projects, the EDP and the RDIP. Firms may benefit from various other programs that promote productivity growth and that are focused on specific industries, such as the shipbuilding program. Many of these potentially assist labor, especially in structurally depressed industries, to cope with changing market conditions, but there are also a variety of programs that directly aid workers.

The *Manpower Consultative Service* annually helps some 70,000 firms that are anticipating or experiencing employment changes and layoffs as a result of changing technological or market conditions. The program is designed to help labor and management work together to ease burdens and to make full use of government programs. The *Canada Manpower Mobility Program* provides job search and relocation assistance to displaced workers whose skills are not needed close to home. The *Adjustment Assistance Benefits Program* gives income support to workers displaced by imports in the clothing and textile sectors or workers displaced because of government restructuring programs in footwear and tanning industries. During 1979–80, $16 million was spent through these three programs (see Table 16).

Other government programs assisting unemployed workers to obtain new job skills and firms to improve the quality of their workforce may also aid eligible workers adversely affected by structural change to take advantage of new opportunities. Unemployed workers may develop new skills with government-financed training and subsistance allowances through the *Canada Manpower Training Program*. Firms may also apply for wage and training cost subsidies through the *Canada Manpower Industrial Training Program* and the *Critical Trade Skills Program*.

Over the 1981–84 period, these programs will be supplemented by the four-year special *Industry and Labor Adjustment Program*. The labor aspects of this program are

---

49   Ibid.

50   Ibid.

**TABLE 16. EXPENDITURES FOR LABOR-FORCE ADJUSTMENT AND
TRAINING PROGRAMS, 1979–80 ESTIMATES
($ Can. Millions)**

Manpower Consultative Service	3
Canada Manpower Mobility Program	10
Adjustment Assistance Benefits Program	3
Canada Manpower Training Program	
Training Program	346
Subsistance Allowances and Unemployment Insurance	225
Canada Manpower Industrial Training Program	103
Critical Trade Skills Training	n.a.

Source: Ministry of State for Economic Development, *Assistance to Business in Canada* (Ottawa: Supply and Services Canada, 1981).

primarily designed to help unemployed workers in designated areas that have experienced major plant closures as a result of recent changes in market conditions. The enhanced benefits available to workers include training incentives, portable wage subsidies, relocation assistance, and early retirement benefits.

6

Provincial Industrial Policies

Over the past decade or so, the provinces have begun to pursue activist economic development programs that often embody important elements of industrial policy. This has become a source of conflict between the provinces and the federal government and is emerging as a substantial problem for U.S. businesses and officials dealing with Canada in matters of trade and other economic concerns.

The motivations for these provincial policies originate from, among other things:

- views held by many provinces that the most desirable patterns of regional and provincial specialization conflict with those that have emerged, or could potentially emerge, as a result of market forces and federal policies;

- perceptions that federal policies have favored Ontario, or Ontario and Quebec, and have been responsible for a misallocation of economic activity—specifically, a concentration in central Canada of manufacturing and related service activities that generate high quality, well-paying employment opportunities.

Consequently, the provinces, other than Ontario, have been placing demands on the federal government to redress these "imbalances" and, further, have begun to pursue policies that have been characterized as province building at the expense of country building. Meanwhile, Ontario is seeking federal assistance to maintain and modernize its industrial base. These initiatives have led to intense competition among the provinces and to serious strains between them and the federal government.

Knowledgeable observers and high-level policymakers within the federal government are concerned that these provincial policies are eroding the Canadian common market by imposing substantial nontariff barriers to trade among the provinces, as well as with other countries. They are concerned that a necessary federal primacy in the conduct of economic policy is being eroded and must be reasserted.

SPECIALIZATION AND COMPETITION AMONG THE PROVINCES

Natural resource development is prevalent throughout Canada, and all 10 provinces have natural resource-based industries. These industries (e.g., agriculture, forestry and fisheries, oil and gas, and mining) account for about 7 percent of Canada's GNP, while manufacturing contributes about 22 percent. But the latter includes many resource-based processing activities, and semiprocessed materials constitute an important source of Canadian exports. The source of irritation is that most manufacturing activities, especially advanced manufacturing and accompanying business services, are located in southern Ontario and Quebec along a strip running from Windsor to Quebec City. The regional distribution of manufacturing output is as follows:

	Share of Canadian Manufacturing Output, 1979[1] (Percent)
Atlantic	3.8
Quebec	26.8
Ontario	52.1
Prairies	8.1
British Columbia	9.1

Ontario has a diversified economy with strong agricultural and mining sectors and a manufacturing sector that produces a broad range of producer and consumer durable goods. Quebec exports iron ore, forest products and asbestos and has a major manufacturing sector. But Quebec's manufacturing employment, compared to that of Ontario, includes a relatively larger share of traditional labor-intense industries that offer poor growth prospects and are likely to continue declining in relative importance in the future. The other regions of Canada are considerably more dependent than Ontario and Quebec on natural resource and manufacturing activities devoted to the initial processing of these resources. The important resource sectors are forest products and minerals in British Columbia; oil, gas, wheat, beef, and minerals in the Prairie region; fish, some minerals and forest products in the Atlantic provinces.[2]

As Canada developed behind a substantial tariff wall and with a transportation policy to encourage east-west linkages, and as southern Ontario and Quebec emerged as the center of industrial activity, the rest of Canada evolved, more or less, as a market for their products and a source of natural resources. Important financial, commercial and other business service activities naturally became concentrated in Ontario and Quebec.

Over time, many Canadians in the western and Atlantic provinces have become dissatisfied with this arrangement because of the limitations on high quality employment opportunities imposed by this pattern of specialization, the cyclical nature of the prosperity associated with dependence on natural resources and a limited range of manufactured exports, and the significant influence outside decisionmakers (e.g., MNCs) can have on resource development patterns. Further, high tariffs raised the costs of manufactured goods and thereby lowered the terms of trade of these more resource-oriented provinces.

Dissatisfaction in Quebec also stems from a variety of economic factors, but political and cultural factors are probably more important than in the English-speaking provinces. Quebec has a disproportionate share of declining or stagnant industrial activities, is dissatisfied with the degree of diversification achieved in its industrial base, and is unhappy with the amount of processing its natural resources receive before export.

Ontario's problem is somewhat different. Containing more than half of Canada's manufacturing activities, modernization, rather than diversification, is a relatively more important problem than it is in the western and Atlantic provinces. Ontario must rationalize its industry to meet the challenges of trade liberalization and competition from other advanced industrial countries and new industrial centers in the Third

---

1   The Conference Board of Canada, *Quarterly Provincial Forecast,* 1980 edition.

2   Judith Maxwell and Caroline Pestieau, *Economic Realities of Canadian Contemporary Confederation* (Montreal: C.D. Howe Research Institute, 1980), pp. 79–81.

World. It is doing this in an era in which the other provinces are lobbying the federal government to pursue policies that disperse industry and are encouraging this process by becoming increasingly involved in competitive policies to attract industrial activity.

To some degree, many of the provinces have policy objectives similar to the national industrial goals described in Chapter 4. These objectives include further processing of resources before they are exported, increased manufacturing activity — especially in high technology sectors — and greater participation in various business services. To achieve the diversification of activities and high quality employment opportunities they believe necessary,[3] various provinces are using many industrial policy instruments similar to nontariff barriers to trade, such as financial incentives, public ownership and joint ventures, conditional access to natural resources, and discriminatory procurement policies. As Figure 9 indicates, these practices have created competition for industrial activity in a variety of sectors.

There is a real danger that these policies could lead to the balkanization of the Canadian economy. In the past, a protected Canadian market proved too small to allow sufficient economies of scales for efficient, internationally competitive production in many industries. Further dividing this market would impose enormous efficiency costs on Canadians and make national industrial policy objectives much more difficult to achieve.

Like federal policies, these provincial policies cause U.S. firms to locate activities in Canada and in particular provinces to gain market access. To some extent, U.S. states have participated in kind, creating an atmosphere of intense competition among the states and provinces to attract new industry. This process of competitive bidding for industries imposes substantial costs on all concerned, as much of the industry attracted by one state or province is won at the expense of another. The net effect is to distort the allocation of resources and to reduce economic efficiency in both countries.

From a negotiating perspective, U.S. trade policymakers are faced with the problem of dealing with Canada's federal government about practices that more or less lie outside its jurisdiction or of dealing with 10 provincial governments and the federal government simultaneously.

POLICIES IN ALBERTA, ONTARIO AND QUEBEC[4]

Alberta

Alberta, with only 9 percent of the population, is Canada's major energy-producing province, accounting for about 85 percent of the country's oil and natural gas production and close to 50 percent of its coal production. The province also produces about 20 percent of the nation's agricultural output. Its manufacturing sector is small, contributing only about 9 percent of the province's total output, less than half the national average (see Table 17). Furthermore, food products and petroleum and coal products account for a little over 50 percent of manufacturing shipments.

---

3   These trends are documented in detail in Maxwell and Pestieau, *Economic Realities*, pp. 83–89.

4   A survey of the policies of all 10 provinces is beyond the scope of this study. Alberta, Ontario and Quebec will be examined because of the significant effects their policies may be expected to have on the United States.

FIGURE 9. SOME AREAS OF PROVINCIAL COMPETITION FOR INDUSTRIAL ACTIVITY

Petrochemicals:	Ontario, Quebec, and Alberta have all laid claim to a world-scale petrochemical complex. In the early 1970s, Alberta attempted to use its bargaining power with respect to energy supplies to obtain federal support for a petrochemical complex. In the end several plants were started with support from the Alberta government. Quebec believes that the national oil policy of the 1960s created an unfair advantage for Sarnia over Montreal. In fact, Sarnia appears to have a distinct market advantage over both Montreal and Alberta as a result of its location close to major U.S. markets.
Steel:	Most of the provinces aspire to having a steel-making complex. Quebec has invested millions of dollars in SIDBEC, a crown corporation that is struggling to reduce a large operating deficit. Nova Scotia has initiated numerous studies of a new steel complex to replace the antiquated steel mill in Sydney, but these plans have been set aside in view of the worldwide problem of excess steel-making capacity. British Columbia and Alberta have also expressed an interest in establishing an integrated steel industry.
Auto assembly:	The Quebec government has been outraged by federal support for Ontario's successful bid to attract the Ford Motor Company of Canada, Limited, engine plant to Windsor, Ontario,[a] and has bid to attract bus assembly and auto parts plants to Quebec.
Deep-water ports:	Nova Scotia opposed a New Brunswick application to the National Energy Board for permission to build a deep-water port in order to handle liquified natural gas (LNG) for delivery to the eastern United States.[b] Quebec has also expressed an interest in constructing LNG port facilities.
Oceanography:	Nova Scotia and British Columbia both aspire to being the national center for cold-water oceanographic research and are urging the federal government to provide support.

[a]Letter from the Hon. Rodrigue Tremblay, Quebec Minister of Industry and Commerce, to the Hon. Jack Horner, federal Minister of Industry, Trade and Commerce, November 30, 1978.
[b]National Energy Board, *Reasons for Decision in the Matter of Applications under the National Energy Board Act of Tenneco LNG Inc., Canadian Lowell Gas Ltd., Lorneterm LNG Limited, and TransCanada PipeLines (New Brunswick) Limited* (Ottawa, 1977).

Source: Judith Maxwell and Caroline Pestieau, *Economic Realities of Contemporary Confederation* (Montreal: C.D. Howe Research Institute, 1980), Table 13, p. 85. Reproduced with permission.

Alberta's development policy is to encourage resource extraction, resource processing and diversification into other sectors.

The province owns the basic rights to its mineral resources and has encouraged their development through what it considers to be favorable royalty rates. So that revenues generated by this development may benefit future generations of Albertans, a substantial share of the resulting earnings are deposited in the Alberta Heritage Savings Trust Fund. The fund is being used to invest in enterprises that will strengthen and diversify Alberta's economy, to invest in energy development and commercial ventures throughout Canada, to make loans directly to or guaranteed by the other provinces and the federal government, and to invest in public capital projects in Alberta that do not necessarily generate returns. (The last two activities are each restricted to no more than 20 percent of the fund.) As of March 31, 1981, the province had invested 53

TABLE 17. COMPOSITION OF PROVINCIAL OUTPUT, 1979
(Percentages of Total Provincial Output)

	Primary[1]	Manufacturing	Construction & Utilities	Services[2]
Newfoundland	15.6	11.0	18.1	55.2
Prince Edward Island	9.3	8.1	10.9	71.3
Nova Scotia	6.3	14.8	10.0	68.8
New Brunswick	6.0	15.4	12.9	65.7
Quebec	3.5	24.9	9.7	61.9
Ontario	2.9	29.0	7.0	61.1
Manitoba	7.9	14.8	8.3	69.0
Saskatchewan	26.8	6.3	11.2	55.7
Alberta	18.6	8.7	15.7	56.9
British Columbia, Yukon and Northwest Territories	7.1	17.5	9.6	65.7
Canada	6.7	22.0	9.5	61.7

[1]Agriculture, forestry, fishing, and mining.
[2]Includes government activities.
Source: The Conference Board of Canada, *Quarterly Provincial Forecast*, 1980 edition.

percent of its funds in ventures to strengthen and diversify Alberta's economy and 0.3 percent in energy ventures, loaned 17 percent to the rest of Canada, and invested 11 percent in public capital projects. The balance of the fund's assets, 18 percent, were in other portfolio investments.[5]

To achieve the maximum possible economic benefits from resource development, the province is encouraging increased processing of fossil fuels, forest products and other resources in Alberta. Further, it is trying to foster the development of a diversified manufacturing sector to ensure employment opportunities when the oil resource is depleted. Some of the main areas of interest are:

- food processing;
- petrochemicals;
- forest products;
- synthetic crude oil;
- machinery—especially for agriculture, oil and gas extraction, petrochemical plants, and oil refineries;
- high technology and R&D-intense activities; and
- financial services (e.g., encouraging financial institutions to locate facilities in Alberta).

To implement this strategy, Alberta's Conservative government has generally opposed direct grants but has used other industrial policy tools. Its efforts to encourage investment are at times very complex, and only some of the more important can be described here.

- The province is involved in joint ventures through the Alberta Heritage Savings Trust Fund. The AHSTF owns 50 percent of the Alberta Energy Company, which in turn

5   As of March 31, 1981, the fund already had $8.9 billion in assets. See *Alberta Heritage Savings Trust Fund Annual Report*, August 1980. One estimate indicates these may grow to $20 billion by 1985, a staggering amount considering Alberta's population is only about 2 million. See Ian Brown, "The $7-Billion Strategy," *Saturday Night* (December 1980).

owns 20 percent of the Syncrude Project at Mildred Lake, part of a coal mine near Robb and part of a forest products complex in the Whitecourt-Fox Creek area. The AHSTF also directly owns about 8 percent equity in the Syncrude Project, which produced about 17 million barrels in 1979–80, its first full year of operation.

• NOVA, an Alberta corporation, has a monopoly within the province on the transportation of natural gas. It is wholly privately owned, but some of its directors are appointed by the government from the private sector. Once gas has entered into the pipeline system, NOVA's subsidiary—Alberta Gas Ethylene Company Ltd.—has a monopoly on the right to extract ethane. The province's ability to ensure a supply of this petrochemical feedstock, along with the favorable natural gas prices mandated by federal regulations, have helped the province to encourage petrochemical manufacturing in Alberta.

• The Alberta Opportunity Company provides loans and loan guarantees to small businesses unable to obtain credit from other sources.

• AHSTF is subsidizing medical and oil sands R&D through ventures such as the Alberta Foundation for Medical Research Endowment Fund, the Walter C. MacKenzie Health Sciences Center and the Alberta Oil Sands Technology and Research Authority.

• The province also encourages R&D through the Canada/Alberta Energy Resources Research Fund—a federal-provincial project that conducts research through contracts with private firms and grants to universities—and the Alberta Research Council, which provides technical and engineering information services and undertakes contract research.

• Alberta is encouraging the increased processing of its forest resources through Forest Management Agreements with the private sector in return for perpetual cutting rights in specified forest areas.

• Alberta provides 50 percent of the funds for three technical assistance programs designed to help firms improve their management skills, develop their export markets and, in areas where federal aid is not available, design or redesign products.[6]

• Of particular significance to U.S. firms is Alberta's policy of maximizing the Albertan/Canadian content of all projects requiring Industrial Development Permits, Forest Management Agreements, or Oil Sands, Power Plants or Coal Development Permits. On construction projects, the Minister of State for Economic and Regional Development must be satisfied with the use, where practical, of Alberta professional services, labor force, materials, and equipment. In practice this policy requires firms to:

–locate procurement offices in Alberta;

–specify in advance the degree of Canadian content that can be achieved and adhere to it throughout the project;

–seek out all potential Canadian suppliers and, when requested, add Canadian firms to bid lists;

–develop objective methods for selecting suppliers and justify their choices if a private-sector complaint is made;

–accept arbitration if the government disagrees with the choice of a contractor.

It is not clear that Alberta has a comparative advantage in all of the industries it wishes to promote. Yet, far from the continent's principal markets, the province is not

---

6   These are the Management Assistance Program, the Market Development Assistance Program and the Product Design and Marketing Program.

satisfied with the employment and investment opportunities afforded its citizens by its natural areas of specialization—resource extraction with some accompanying industrialization.

Ontario

Historically, Canada's high levels of protection and its transportation policy designed to build up east-west market linkages were strong stimuli to industrial development in Ontario. This province is the industrial heartland of Canada, accounting for more than 50 percent of the country's manufacturing with only about 36 percent of its population. Manufacturing accounts for 29 percent of Ontario's total output—significantly above the national average of 22 percent—while extractive industries contribute only 3 percent—below the national average of 7 percent (see Table 17). Having the largest manufacturing sector in Canada, Ontario confronts the full range of Canadian industrial policy problems described in Chapter 4.

- Ontario must restructure its industry to meet the challenges of trade liberalization and higher energy prices and to take advantage of new export opportunities in a low growth environment. Many of its industries must be rationalized by increasing production runs, and its largest industry, automobiles, faces most of the same long-term structural adjustments as does its U.S. counterpart.

- Containing much of Canada's manufacturing, Ontario has a great deal to lose from the gradual erosion of the Canadian common market. Policies that maintain free access to markets in other provinces (as well as relatively good access to adjacent U.S. markets) offer the best opportunities for the continued growth of Ontario's industry.

Ontario's interests are best served by federal industrial development policies designed to foster adjustment, the development of new industries, R&D-intense activities, and the like without attempting to achieve a desired regional distribution of industrial activity. The converse is true of federal efforts to subsidize the regional redistribution of industrial activity, especially when these efforts may be made at the cost of economic efficiency.

In this environment, the Ontario government is undertaking certain programs to strengthen existing industries and to exploit future opportunities.[7]

- Ontario is encouraging the maintenance of a common market among the provinces protected by discriminatory domestic procurement practices. It sees provincial barriers to trade within Canada as counterproductive and suggests that the provinces encourage Canadian sourcing in general. Ontario provides a 10 percent procurement preference for Canadian goods and its Ministry of Industry and Tourism is pursuing other ambitious programs to encourage Canadian sourcing. These include:

---

7 The observations that follow are based on the authors' interpretations of *The Opening Remarks of the Hon. Larry Grossman At the Estimates of the Ministry of Industry and Tourism,* October 1980. Also see *Supplementary Measures to Stimulate the Economy,* Economic Statement by the Honorable Frank S. Miller, Treasurer of Ontario, November 13, 1980.

-promotional programs to encourage consumers to select Canadian goods;
-import replacement programs to make manufacturers aware of Ontario's suppliers;
-Canadian sourcing requirements for firms receiving industrial incentive grants;
-activities to persuade other Ontario agencies and the federal government to source from Ontario firms;
-cooperative Canadian sourcing ventures with other provinces.

- Ontario has an active export promotion program, including:
  -export credits;
  -trade promotion activities — 38 trade missions and participation in trade fairs;
  -special programs to assist small businesses;
  -legal services to assist firms faced by legal constraints — quotas, product standards and licensing arrangements;
  -assistance to firms in forming consortiums to bid on large foreign contracts.

- Ontario is providing industrial incentives on a selective basis.
  -During 1979–81, the Employment Development Fund (EDF) provided grants to firms to help improve the province's competitive position and long-term development prospects. The EDF's activities were directed by a Cabinet committee, which has been replaced by a new committee responsible for coordinating economic development policy, the Board of Industrial Leadership and Development.

  -Ontario's Economic Development Corporation provides loans and loan guarantees to small businesses and supports a foreign subsidiary buy-back program.

- Ontario is encouraging research and development and R&D-intense activities.
  -The Ontario Research Foundation undertakes R&D projects that help Ontario firms develop new products. For example, it conducts product development research for small firms that cannot afford to establish permanent ongoing research facilities.

  -Further, the province provides financial incentives to firms to locate R&D facilities in Ontario.

- Ontario has programs to assist restructuring in the automobile and pulp and paper industries.

- Ontario is actively seeking new, including foreign, investment. However, it is looking for MNCs that will grant their Ontario subsidiaries global product mandates.

On November 13, 1980, the Ontario government announced the establishment of the Board of Industrial Leadership and Development, a Cabinet committee, to coordinate Ontario's economic development efforts and to serve as economic liaison with the federal government. On January 27, 1981, Ontario's Premier, William G. Davis, unveiled BILD's $1.5 billion five-year economic development program. The program stresses the importance of developing a variety of high technology activities, including major nuclear energy projects, initiatives to encourage natural resource development, and transportation infrastructure investments. It is hoped that these projects will help create markets for certain high technology Ontario industries—e.g., nuclear power technology, mass transportation equipment and resource extraction machinery. The program also incorporates incentives for the use of electric vehicles and nonpetroleum fuels, which, combined with the accelerated development of nuclear power, are to encourage the use of hydrogen as an auto fuel. The province has entered into a joint venture with the Canada Development Corporation and John Labatt Ltd. to establish Allelix, Inc., a biotechnology company. It also hopes to obtain other industrial spinoffs by establishing research facilities in microelectronics, auto parts and computer-assisted manufacturing. In addition, Ontario plans to increase financial assistance to emerging small high technology firms.

Ontario's fiscal capacity is limited, but it has already committed $800 million to the five-year program. Ontario is seeking assistance from Ottawa to help finance the program.[8]

Quebec

Quebec produces about 26 percent of Canada's manufactures with approximately the same share of the country's population. Manufacturing accounts for 25 percent of Quebec's total output—above the national average of 22 percent—while extractive activities account for only about 4 percent—below the national average of 7 percent (see Table 17). During the 1960s and 1970s, Quebec's share of the nation's manufacturing activity declined. And during the last decade, this trend contributed to a growing unemployment problem. From 1969 to 1980, the labor force grew at 2.5 percent a year while employment grew only 2.1 percent a year.

Structural weaknesses in the manufacturing sector have been important. As noted, Quebec has a disproportionate share of the nation's labor-intense industries (e.g., textiles, apparel, leather goods, and furniture) that are likely to continue declining as competition from newly industrializing countries intensifies. Further, the growth of manufacturing activities dependent on forest resources will be constrained by physical limitations. However, Quebec possesses a sound foundation of high technology activities upon which it can build future industrial growth—aeronautics, transportation equipment, communications equipment, electronic products. Further, its substantial hydroelectric resources should allow its leadership in aluminum (about 75 percent of Canada's production) to continue and to experience substantial growth in energy-intense activities, such as electrometallurgical, electrochemical and some branches of nonmetallic manufacturing.

Many officials in the provincial government believe that the French culture has been a partial barrier to the entrance of Francophones into the mainstream of Canada's business and professional communities, inhibiting the development of indigenous entrepreneurial and managerial skills. In the past, French-speaking entrepreneurs and private-sector managers have tended to be concentrated in small enterprises that produce for local markets or in traditional sectors. Also until recently, in the

---

8   As discussed in Chapter 5, the federal government's capacity to undertake new initiatives is limited, and political pressure for assistance to other provinces is strong. Yet, Ontario officials remain hopeful that Ottawa will be able to provide some help.

more dynamic industries, Francophones were more often found in government-owned enterprises than in the private sector. Therefore, Quebec has placed as much emphasis on the development of the entrepreneurial and managerial capacities within its indigenous firms and labor force as it has on its sectoral objectives.

More than any other province, Quebec has an explicit industrial policy. The province's overall economic policy is laid out in *Bâtir le Québec: Énoncé de politique économique.*[9] This is a clear attempt to provide a public blueprint of the ways in which provincial policies are to be harmonized and coordinated to create, foster and achieve a desired course of industrial development within the constraints and opportunities created by federal domestic and international economic policies and the domestic and international environments. It is a clear assertion of the present government's intention to intervene. "It is the government's intention to promote the redeployment of the forces of the economy on the basis of policy objectives and specific measures affecting the various economic sectors: agriculture, fishing, forestry, mineral resources, etc."[10]

The policy statement provides an analysis of the weaknesses within the Quebec economy and the historical causes of these problems. It cites chronic unemployment and the inadequacies of the present industrial base. No small share of the blame for the underemployment of the province's economic potential is placed on federal domestic and international economic policies and the extensive external control of Quebec enterprises.

The policy statement lays out objectives and instruments that focus on both the performance of firms in general and individual sectors.

The program is designed to assist and encourage firms, improve marketing and entrepreneurial skills and labor-management relations; increase R&D; form industry cooperatives; and, where appropriate, achieve mergers.

At the sectoral levels, the policy statement focuses on the need to increase processing of Quebec's natural resources and to accelerate the development of industries in which Quebec has a comparative advantage. The sectors identified as having promising opportunities include:

- food and agriculture (beef cattle, grain for fodder, truck farming);
- maritime fishing;
- forestry;
- mineral resource-based activities;
- electricity-intense manufacturing—e.g., aluminum, magnesium, glass;
- industries in which Quebec has an unusual base of human capital—e.g., heavy electrical equipment, mass transportation equipment, aerospace equipment; and
- tourism.

The statement also stresses the need to support basic industries in which Quebec lacks a comparative advantage. The statement notes that other countries support

---

9   Government of Quebec, *Challenges for Quebec: A Statement on Economic Policy* (1979). As this study went to press, Quebec released volume II of this plan, *Le Virage Technologique: Bâtir le Québec—Phase 2, Programme d'action économique 1982–1986*, which laid out a detailed blueprint and five-year plan for the development of its high technology sectors.

10   Government of Quebec, *Challenges for Quebec*, p. 91.

these sectors and states that a Quebec presence in these sectors is necessary to assure a balanced economy. Petrochemicals, other chemicals and steel fall in this category.

Finally, the policy statement makes it clear that Quebec does not intend to abandon less competitive sectors such as textiles and leather goods. Discussions with Quebec officials indicate a skepticism about the adjustment process—the capacity of workers and firms to move into the more promising sectors. Further, while expressing the need to foster growth in the more sophisticated branches of manufacturing, these officials expressed the need to find ways to rationalize and make these industries more competitive. Quebec will likely sustain pressure on the federal government to maintain protection for these industries. However, discussions with Quebec officials indicate that the overall objective is to maintain employment, so that over time with a growing economy, the relative importance of these sectors declines.

Quebec employs a variety of industrial policy tools that are too numerous to catalogue here.[11] The following list of provincial programs, however, should indicate how extensive the province's activities are.

- Quebec has an ambitious buy provincial program that includes price preferences for Quebec suppliers.

- Quebec provides financial incentives for industrial activities through a variety of programs:
    - the Société de développement industriel (SDI) provides subsidies through interest rebates on company loans, and financing through direct loans and equity financing;
    - investment tax credits are available on 25 percent of qualifying investments up to 50 percent of tax liabilities;
    - regional development banks have been established to provide risk capital;
    - sector modernization programs have been established to provide grants in pulp and paper, textiles, forestry, fishing, food and agriculture, furniture, and footwear.

- Through the Société générale de financement (SGF), the province owns stock in a variety of corporations. SGF's holdings cover the full span of manufacturing activities—shipbuilding, electrical machinery, petrochemicals, and many others. Quebec is also a steel producer through Sidbec.

- Quebec is rationing access to its low-priced hydroelectric power to large industrial users on the basis of their overall contribution to the Quebec economy. This program is an effort to require these users to locate in Quebec more than just those aspects of their activities that use electricity intensively.

- The province also has active programs to promote export market development and the application of advanced technologies in Quebec.

This broad range of programs indicates that Quebec is not satisfied to leave industrial policymaking to the federal government alone. The same may be said about

---

11   Quebec spends about 5 percent of its budget on economic development, which is more than any other province; Ontario spends 3.5 percent, for example. See Department of Regional Economic Expansion, *Economic Development Prospects in Quebec* (Ottawa, 1979), p. 33.

the other provinces, although in some cases to a more limited degree. As these sentiments grow, tensions will increase between the federal and provincial government over the leadership role Ottawa has historically assumed in economic policymaking, and interprovincial rivalries will continue to jeopardize the integrity of the Canadian common market.

7

The Outlook for Canadian Industrial Policy

Within Canada today, there are several competing points of view about the desired direction for Canadian policy. This debate is inducing a serious reexamination of many important policies and programs that will shape Canada's overall industrial strategy for the next 10 to 20 years. It is taking place in the context of two important sets of domestic and international realities.

First, Canada is committed to full participation in the Tokyo Round tariff reductions (1980–87) and to implementation of the GATT codes governing nontariff barriers. To the extent required by these agreements, therefore, Canada will be exposing its industry to more foreign competition as well as to increased export opportunities.

Second, since the late 1960s, federal government intervention and participation in the operation of the domestic economy has increased. In particular, this has taken the form of regulation of foreign investment, provision of financial and tax incentives for R&D and industrial development, public ownership of market-sector enterprises and venture capital firms, the strategic uses of the price of energy and government procurement, and efforts to encourage Canadian sourcing in the private sector. This activist trend is also apparent in provincial policies, although these may at times work at cross-purposes with federal policies.

Discussions about the desired direction and rate of change for these policies have generated alternative policy prescriptions that vary along two axes. Specifically, they differ in their recommendations concerning trade liberalization and intervention in the domestic economy. So viewed, the present array of prescriptions may be divided into three broad types of approaches:

- freer trade/domestic noninterventionist;
- interventionist (on both counts); and
- freer trade/domestic interventionist.

Proponents of these alternative approaches agree to some extent on the general characteristics of Canada's economic problems—a fragmented structure of production in manufacturing that must be rationalized, insufficient Canadian participation in the production and processing of its natural resources, a growing negative trade balance in finished manufactured goods, and inadequate levels of domestic development and application of advanced technologies in manufacturing. Where they differ substantially is in the remedies they prescribe for dealing with these concerns.

The rest of this chapter is divided into two parts. The first describes the three different types of approaches to industrial policy that are being advocated by various government ministers and officials, private-sector decisionmakers, and professionals and intellectuals. The second describes the politically and economically feasible changes that may be made in the international and domestic industrial policy instruments described in Chapter 5 and examines the likely future course of Canadian policy.

COMPETING APPROACHES TO INDUSTRIAL POLICY

Freer Trade/Domestic Noninterventionist Approach[1]

Proponents of this approach favor a gradual reduction of trade barriers through multilateral and bilateral negotiations, coupled with short-term safeguards and adjustment assistance for firms and individuals adversely affected by trade. In the long run, they favor reliance on market forces to determine the types of goods Canada produces, imports and exports, as opposed to a systematic government strategy to guide the structure of development.[2]

In general, this group welcomes the progress made in the Tokyo Round and would be favorably disposed toward further negotiations to obtain additional access to foreign markets. Advocates would place primary emphasis on the positive effects of the competition that reciprocal free trade would generate in formulating an industrial policy.

It is this group's view that Canada's structural economic problems have their root causes in the limited size of the Canadian market. They believe that the progress of the Canadian manufacturing sector has been limited by a lack of guaranteed free access to larger markets that Japanese, European and U.S. producers have enjoyed, either from a large domestic population or the Common Market. At the same time, high Canadian tariffs have permitted a relatively inefficient industrial structure to survive. In their view, multilateral and bilateral liberalization would provide Canadian industry with larger markets and the ability to achieve greater industrial specialization and economies of scale. Further, they do not necessarily see foreign investment or the lack of an activist industrial policy as the primary source of Canada's difficulties.

Interventionist Approach

Opposite the first group are advocates of industrial policies that would rationalize Canadian industry and build international competitiveness through government initiatives and incentives. Many proponents of this approach believe that the high level of foreign ownership and the large number of foreign subsidiaries in Canada are an important source of Canada's structural problems in industry. They are generally ambivalent toward trade liberalization and advocate maintaining protection, at least until Canadian industry has achieved levels of productivity and the specialization necessary to compete in world markets. A variety of policies along such lines have been prescribed, all seeming to share a reluctance to rely on the market forces generated by trade liberalization—that is, import competition and export opportunities—to generate a desirable reorganization of Canadian industry. Rather, they propose to have the govern-

---

1   This type of prescription has often been referred to as outward looking. Studies reflecting some elements of this approach include: Economic Council of Canada, *Looking Outward: A New Trade Strategy for Canada* (Ottawa, 1975); Donald J. Daly, "Lagging Productivity Growth: Causes and Remedies" (York University, July 1979, mimeo); Paul and Ronald Wonnacott, "Free Trade Between the United States and Canada Fifteen Years Later" (University of Maryland Working Paper, March 1980). These and other proponents differ somewhat in their policy prescriptions, and the characterization of their approach here is not intended to be a representation of the views of any one author.

2   It is important to point out, however, that these proponents would not necessarily oppose regional or industry assistance that helps compensate for market imperfections and other institutional barriers to development.

ment participate in the selection of industries and activities that may eventually become internationally competitive.

An important example of this type of approach is the technology-oriented policies espoused in two recent Science Council publications. The first, by John Britton and James Gilmour, is an assessment of Canada's economic problems that advocates a technologically oriented industrial policy. This policy prescription is further illuminated in a report of the Science Council Industrial Policies Committee (SCIP).[3]

According to Britton and Gilmour, it is not protection but the high level of foreign ownership and large number of foreign subsidiaries in Canada that have led to Canada's structural problems. They believe that foreign ownership tends to result in the location of R&D, product design and marketing and other professional and planning activities outside Canada. They feel this retards the development of the Canadian capacity to undertake these important activities and puts Canadian industry in a poor position to move into the high technology, sophisticated branches of manufacturing and service activities that provide the best growth opportunities for advanced industrial countries. Britton and Gilmour believe foreign firms further contribute to Canada's balance-of-trade problems by being more inclined to import components and services than are domestic firms and by being less likely to export.

They view Canada as thus industrially underdeveloped because it relies too much on raw material exports to pay for its imports; relies too much on imports of manufactured goods; relies too much on imported technology; and lacks the innovative and technological capacity to expand its exports in high technology goods and services, as exports of resource products become less capable of paying for imports.

The SCIP proposes a policy to restructure the Canadian economy with emphasis on high technology industries. While acknowledging that negotiated trade agreements potentially provide tremendous opportunity to expand markets, the SCIP cautions that agreements should be negotiated with Canada's strengths and weaknesses in mind—although it is not specific about how this is to be achieved. The proposed industrial policy is very nationalistic, relies extensively on government intervention to correct existing problems and guide future development, and favors domestic producers over foreign suppliers.

The SCIP program's overall goal is technological sovereignty, and it has four main components:

- increasing the demand for Canadian technology by means such as directing government procurement toward more highly innovative firms;

- expanding Canada's potential to develop technology by providing a favorable investment environment; by sponsoring the expansion of core firms likely to lead technological innovation in particular industries; by encouraging mergers and joint ventures to achieve necessary economies of scale; and by other means;

- strengthening the capacity of firms for technological absorption by, for example, developing links between small and medium-size firms and universities and research centers;

---

3   John N.H. Britton and James M. Gilmour, *The Weakest Link: A Technological Perspective on Canadian Industrial Underdevelopment* (Ottawa: Science Council, 1978) and Science Council, *Forging the Links: A Technology Policy for Canada* (Ottawa, 1979).

- encouraging MNCs to import technology on terms favorable to Canada's industrial policy objectives, such as Canadian participation in product development and exports. This could be achieved by means such as performance requirements and encouraging global product mandates.

Freer Trade/Domestic Interventionist Approach

Standing somewhere between the two groups just discussed are advocates of a further gradual reduction of trade barriers—or at least of an acceptance of those agreed to in the Tokyo Round—with adjustment assistance for Canadian workers displaced by imports. But they also believe that concerted and coordinated government efforts are necessary to ensure that Canadian industry exploits the opportunities created by multilateral tariff reductions. It is their view that various types of domestic intervention—e.g., adjustment assistance and industrial incentives—are necessary to ensure that, as trade barriers are reduced, the economy is restructured to be internationally competitive in a manner consistent with Canadian objectives. Of course, these domestic policies may indirectly distort trade, undoing some of the liberalization achieved through multilateral negotiations.

Although this group acknowledges the positive contribution made by foreign capital and technology to Canadian economic development, it favors measures that seek to ensure the participation of foreign-owned and -controlled firms to some extent in the Canadian economy in accord with Canadian national interests.

Many influential policy advisers appear to embrace important elements of this view, and the policies of the current government as well as previous Trudeau governments reflect this approach in numerous ways. Specifically, the Tokyo Round negotiations were entered into and undertaken by previous Trudeau governments, so the results are taken as given: Canada will reduce its tariffs by an average of about 40 percent between 1980 and 1987 and has taken appropriate steps to implement the new GATT codes governing NTBs in areas such as government procurement, product standards and customs valuation.[4]

Paralleling these efforts to liberalize international trade, the present and predecessor Trudeau governments have supported domestic programs that seek to promote structural adjustment in trade-impacted industries, desirable patterns of new industrial development and regional equity in economic development. Since assuming office for the first time in 1968, Trudeau governments have reorganized existing programs and institutions into new ones and established additional entities. Among these are:

- Department of Regional Economic Expansion (including the Regional Development Incentives Program), 1969;
- Department of Industry, Trade and Commerce, 1969;
- Export Development Corporation, 1970;
- Ministry of State for Science and Technology, 1971;
- Program for Export Market Development, 1971;
- Promotional Projects Program, 1974;
- Shipbuilding Industry Assistance Program, 1975;
- Federal Business Development Bank, 1975;
- Enterprise Development Program, 1977;

---

4 Of course, there is room for interpretation about the constraints imposed by the codes governing NTBs.

- Ministry of State for Economic Development, 1978 (renamed the Ministry of State for Economic and Regional Development with expanded responsibilities in 1982);
- National Energy Program, 1980;
- (Federal) Procurement Review Mechanism, 1980;
- Industry and Labor Adjustment Program, 1981–84;
- Canadian Industrial Renewal Board, 1981;
- Committee on Megaproject Industrial and Regional Benefits, 1981;
- Industrial Opportunities Program, 1981;
- Office of Industrial Adjustment Assistance, 1982;
- Department of Regional Industrial Expansion, 1982.

Further, current and past Trudeau governments have acknowledged the positive role played by foreign capital and technology:

Canada has historically benefited to a substantial degree from the application of foreign capital to our economic life. For the future, the government expects that although Canada has a growing capacity to finance its own investment requirements, foreign capital and technology will continue to play an important role in Canada's economic development in the 1980s and beyond.[5]

Yet, these governments have taken steps to ensure that new foreign investments will serve Canada's national interests and to increase, on a selective basis, Canadian ownership and control. These include the creation of the Canada Development Corporation in 1971, FIRA in 1973, and PetroCan in 1975; and the Canadianization aspects of the National Energy Program, 1980.

OPTIONS AND OUTLOOK FOR CANADIAN INDUSTRIAL POLICY

The coordination of the various Canadian industrial policies and programs into a consistent and explicit policy or strategy, with specific goals and objectives for patterns of industrial development, would require the federal government publicly to pick winners, and by default losers. The Trudeau government does not appear inclined to take that kind of initiative, at least for the time being. To be sure, since assuming power in March 1980, the current government has taken or announced new policy initiatives, including a 31 percent increase in economic and regional development envelope expenditures in 1981–82 and a reorganization of key government departments. But when viewed in the context of all the varied elements that compose Canada's industrial policy, Canada's approach is not likely to become *suddenly* more or less interventionist. Rather, the debate concerns the pace and direction of change and how available resources may be used most effectively through better coordination of existing as well as new programs. The long-term consequences of these activities are still unclear, and some of them have been specified only in general terms.

At the present time, even though the economic and regional development envelope funds have been increased, fiscal constraints limit the government's prospects that large additional resources will be available for economic development. Thus, changes in R&D and industrial incentive programs will focus mostly on better

---

5   Government of Canada, *Economic Development for Canada in the 1980s* (Ottawa, November 12, 1981), p. 12.

coordination and more efficient use of already budgeted funds. The new Industrial Opportunities Program exemplifies such an initiative for R&D programs, as does the Canadian Industrial Renewal Board for industrial development programs. Any further new initiatives will likely be oriented toward leveraging private resources. Examples include encouraging foreign-owned firms to undertake activities consistent with Canadian industrial policy objectives through FIRA reviews and persuading foreign and Canadian firms to purchase more Canadian goods and services. Increased Canadian sourcing could prove particularly useful in fostering the development of high technology capital goods and service industries.

The remainder of this chapter focuses on prospects for Canadian policies in eight areas: international trade, foreign direct investment, energy, competition, R&D incentives, industrial incentives, public enterprises, and procurement.

Trade Policies

Canada's trade policy options are circumscribed by its commitments under the GATT. Its initiatives in this area are further constrained by their high visibility in the United States, which accounts for 70 percent of Canada's trade.

The immediate agenda involves implementing commitments made in the Tokyo Round, where Canada agreed to reduce its tariffs on industrial commodities by an average of about 40 percent between 1980 and 1987. As with all countries, however, the implications of Canada's commitments to the codes governing certain nontariff barriers are less precise at this time. Their coverage is limited, their language is quite general, and their effectiveness in constraining the behavior of all industrial countries remains largely unknown until a body of case law develops from the adjudication of complaints. Canada, like the United States, can choose how vigorously to encourage implementation and strict interpretation of the codes. This choice will thus contribute to determining how strong a basis emerges for effective rules to help ensure more open multilateral trade.

As for further trade liberalization to achieve greater Canadian access to foreign markets, negotiations would necessarily focus less on tariffs than on nontariff barriers, which are rapidly becoming the principal obstacles to the movement of goods. Here, Canada can pursue multilateral agreements or bilateral ones with the United States. The multilateral approach probably best serves Canada's interests since it would provide greater benefits in terms of efficiency gains and tend to lessen Canada's trade dependence on the United States—quite apart from avoiding the complications of establishing new preferential arrangements at a time when the world trading system is losing its multilateral discipline.

Nevertheless, the possibility exists that Canada could negotiate some form of more open trading arrangement solely with the United States. Indeed, some knowledgeable Canadians believe it is logical to focus Canadian trade policy largely on the United States.[6]

U.S.-Canada bilateral trade initiatives might seek agreements along one of three broad approaches:

---

6   See especially Rodney de C. Grey, *Trade Policy in the 1980s: An Agenda for Canadian-U.S. Relations* (Montreal: C.D. Howe Institute, 1981). One of Grey's guiding propositions states that "Multilaterally negotiated solutions are not necessarily the only, or the best, solutions to trade problems between Canada and the United States. On certain issues or in certain situations, Canadians may do better by seeking solutions when not all the other players are at the table"(p. 9).

(1) an extension of each country's multilateral agreements under the Tokyo Round on a strictly bilateral basis. This could center on certain of the new codes that limit the use of nontariff measures, tightening their conduct requirements and/or broadening their coverage;

(2) a limited preferential arrangement, eliminating all or most trade barriers in a particular sector or over a selected package of products. Like the Automotive Agreement, for which this would be a form of sequel, this approach would likely require a GATT waiver;

(3) a formal customs union or free trade area under GATT rules affecting substantially all bilaterally traded products.[7]

The first approach would probably entail extending, on a bilateral basis, the GATT codes that address key areas of industrial policy. For example, Canadians may be interested in sharpening the bilateral application of the government Procurement, Subsidy/Countervail and Customs Valuation Codes. But an arrangement between only two countries raises questions under GATT law: for instance, would the two be obliged to extend the same or comparable concessions to other signatories of the relevant code? In addition, any meaningful extension of a code's coverage within these two federal nations might require unprecedented and certainly difficult negotiations involving commitments from 10 provinces and 50 states.

Traditionally, Canadians have shown interest in the sectoral approach. Candidates for such an agreement include petrochemicals, urban mass transportation equipment and certain high technology electronics industries. The Automotive Agreement set a precedent, but a dubious one, since other sectors encompass far more firms than it did with much more diverse patterns of ownership and involvement in both countries. Thus, firms within them are less likely to reach a consensus favoring such a scheme. And, as was the case with the auto pact, Canada would likely seek to use the agreement to achieve its industrial policy goals by imposing performance requirements on participating U.S. firms in exchange for the benefits of open bilateral trade. However, the U.S. government would probably find these safeguards and performance requirements less acceptable now than when it negotiated the Auto Agreement in 1965.

The third approach, a comprehensive free-trade agreement, may still be thought of as theoretically eliminating only tariffs affecting bilateral trade. But considering how important nontariff trade distortions have become, a truly effective agreement would have to encompass both tariffs and nontariff barriers. This initiative would require extension of the GATT codes on a bilateral basis and, to avoid trade distortions, coordination of some key areas of industrial policy such as some aspects of regional aid, R&D and industrial subsidies, and government procurement. In addition to the problems of negotiating with the states and provinces, this type of agreement would constrain Canadian policy in areas (e.g., subsidies) in which decisionmakers would like to have more freedom of action. Further, the need for policy harmonization would generate domestic political opposition in Canada because of fears of U.S. domination of the decisionmaking process. Finally, for the next several years, the present Liberal government will likely be too preoccupied with dealing with the structural changes necessitated by the Tokyo Round tariff reductions and energy prices to embark on ne-

---

7   These three approaches and the specific issues each might raise are discussed in detail in "Canada-U.S. Free Trade: What Should We Really Be Talking About?", by Sperry Lea for the Council on Foreign Relations, forthcoming 1982.

gotiations that would cause such a fundamental change in the U.S.-Canadian economic relationship.

Policies toward Foreign Direct Investment

As noted earlier in this chapter and discussed in Chapter 5, the current government has postponed its promised expansion of FIRA's mandate, and for the time being FIRA reviews will remain limited to new foreign investments and takeovers of existing enterprises.

As Chapter 5 reported, generating additional exports and enhancing technological development were among the least cited reasons for approving foreign investments by FIRA over the period from 1974–75 to date. However, encouraging additional exports and research and development were the two criteria explicitly mentioned in the government's November 1981 statement of economic development.

> The government's objective is to ensure that foreign-controlled corporations and their Canadian counterparts alike contribute fully to the development of an innovative and internationally competitive industrial structure, pursuing Canadian objectives in areas such as research and development and international marketing with equal vigour. The guiding principle of FIRA is that foreign investment must be of significant benefit to Canada. It is a principle that should be easily adhered to by good corporate citizens.[8]

This may signal a change in emphasis in FIRA reviews that would be consistent with the concept of encouraging global product mandates. As foreign MNCs rationalize their Canadian operations in the 1980s, they may merely produce fewer product lines and maintain central management, product development and international marketing activities outside Canada, if this has been their pattern in the past. Conversely, the Canadian subsidiary may be given a global product mandate with responsibility to undertake the full range of activities, including product development and international marketing, for a specified product line. Advocates of this approach believe the resulting patterns of rationalization would benefit Canadian industry's long-term dynamic competitive position.[9]

Energy Policies

The Canadian government is pursuing an energy program on the premise that it can indeed keep oil and gas prices below world levels, share in the considerable revenues generated by domestic oil sales, and increase Canadian ownership and control of Canadian energy resources without substantially reducing energy development activity. So, for the next several years, Canadian energy prices will probably stay below U.S. prices and continue to provide Canada with an advantage in energy-intense industries.

The Canadianization aspect of the NEP initially made significant progress through the acquisitions of controlling interests of Petrofina Canada, Aquitaine and Hudson's Bay Oil and Gas by Canadian firms. Through these acquisitions and others,

---

8   Government of Canada, *Economic Development*, p. 13.

9   These issues are discussed in more detail in a forthcoming study by Harold Crookell for the Canadian-American Committee.

Canadian ownership increased from 28 percent prior to the NEP to 33 percent as of July 1981.[10] But such acquisitions often strain capital markets and can place substantial downward pressure on the Canadian dollar. Therefore, the Canadian government will likely have to accept slower progress in Canadianization than was achieved in the first nine months after the unveiling of the NEP.

Competition Policies

As discussed in Chapter 5, Canada's antitrust laws are not as restrictive as those of the United States.[11] The present government would like to strengthen certain aspects of these laws, particularly as they relate to monopolies, mergers and collusive agreements, all of which may concentrate market power and thereby reduce competition to the detriment of the public interest.

During the latter part of 1980 and early in 1981, André Ouellet, Minister of Consumer and Corporate Affairs, outlined in public speeches the reforms he would like the government to propose. Ouellet would amend Section 32 of the Combines Investigation Act to prohibit unequivocally price fixing, collective boycotts and market sharing arrangements. He would also place enforcement of Section 33, dealing with mergers and monopolies, under civil law rather than criminal law. Further, he would abandon the "lessening competition to the public detriment" standard in evaluating mergers and monopolies and rely instead on thresholds of market concentration. Finally, he proposes prenotification of mergers to facilitate evaluation and enforcement.

Competition policy is a difficult and politically sensitive area in Canada. Two previous bills to undertake reforms were not successfully legislated and, as of this writing, no new bill has been introduced in Parliament. To the extent that the government is able to move toward stricter control over mergers and the activities of monopolies and oligopolies, legislators or the courts sooner or later will have to face important industrial policy choices with respect to competition from foreign sources.

- First, the government could limit the application of a new, tougher merger law to cases in which more concentrated ownership will not be disciplined by competition from other domestic firms or foreign sources.

- Second, the government could take a more relaxed role about, or in some cases even encourage, mergers, joint ventures and consortiums in industries in which economies of scale are necessary to compete with imports and in foreign markets. Where these include the U.S. market, an affirmative merger policy would have substantial consequences for U.S. MNCs that must deal with the extraterritorial application of U.S. antitrust law.

Research and Development Incentives

There is some concern in Canada that present incentive programs (outlined in Chapter 5) encourage basic research and the preliminary stages of product develop-

---

10   "Canada Pays Price for New Nationalism," *Business Week* (August 17, 1981), p. 40.

11   It should be noted that existing FIRA reviews do provide some check on a class of mergers—those involving acquisitions and other similar arrangements in which one of the parties is deemed to be a nonresident.

ment more than they stimulate adaptation of the new production processes and the production of improved or more advanced products. Therefore, over the next several years, new initiatives will place greater emphasis on encouraging industrial R&D and product development. The federal government hopes to raise Canadian R&D expenditures from about 1.0 to 1.5 percent of GNP by 1985; specifically, it wants to raise industry-funded R&D expenditures from 0.34 to 0.75 percent of GNP.[12]

As discussed earlier in this chapter, some advocates of a strong science policy for Canada have proposed very ambitious initiatives, with an overall goal of technological sovereignty, to be achieved in part through extensive government intervention. This type of interventionist approach is criticized by many professional economists. It involves, like other activist programs, surmounting the political difficulties arising from having to pick winners and losers. Nevertheless, the idea that Canadian R&D efforts need additional government assistance has its supporters, and the present government is committed to pursuing policies that enhance these efforts, although its policies will certainly not be as extreme as some that have been proposed.

Efforts to improve R&D performance will focus on better coordination of programs already in place and leveraging private resources. To get more mileage out of existing federal financial incentives for R&D, the Industrial Opportunities Program will seek to better target available R&D resources to areas perceived to offer the greatest opportunity. By doing so, the government may more effectively articulate its policies toward high technology industries with good growth prospects. In addition, the current government will almost certainly continue to emphasize R&D activity among performance goals for foreign MNCs operating in Canada. Furthermore, as discussed later, encouraging R&D will be among the objectives pursued by the Committee on Megaproject Industrial and Regional Benefits in evaluating firms' applications to participate in oil and gas exploration and development on Canada Lands.

Industrial Incentives

In applying the funds available for economic development and industrial incentives, the government must develop policies for several types of industries:

- industries adversely affected by imports or other structural changes—these include industries in which Canada is at a comparative disadvantage and whose relative importance will decline in the future, and in which Canada may regain lost competitiveness through restructuring;

- mature, internationally competitive industries;

- more sophisticated, high technology industries where substantial growth opportunities are expected for the advanced industrial countries.

The current government is seeking to develop specific policies to assist industries and firms adversely affected by imports and other structural changes. In June 1981, the government announced plans for a special program to assist the textile and apparel firms and workers and committed $250 million to assist firms and workers in adjusting and restructuring to meet the changing competitive environment. The Canadian In-

---

12   Ministry of State for Science and Technology, *R&D Policies, Planning and Programming* (Ottawa, January 1981).

dustrial Renewal Board is being established to coordinate the federal adjustment programs described in Chapter 5 applicable to the apparel, textile and footwear industries.

> The Board will work closely with the firms, workers and communities affected. The Board will have the responsibility for developing industrial renewal plans to provide a longer-term planning framework. It will give particular emphasis to the development of viable firms and the creation of alternative investment and employment opportunities, which will enhance the economic security and future growth prospects of the communities concerned.[13]

Also, as noted in Chapter 5, the special Industry and Labor Adjustment Program will continue (from 1981 to 1984) to provide $350 million of additional assistance to firms in communities adversely affected by plant closures.

Further, in January 1982, the government announced that it is seeking to give its overall adjustment assistance efforts better direction and coordination by establishing an Office of Industrial Adjustment Assistance in the new Department of Regional Industrial Expansion. This office is intended to be the focal point of federal efforts in this area.

Public Enterprises

The role of public enterprises in key sectors, such as energy, transportation and selected areas of manufacturing, to assist in achieving industrial development goals is a well-established practice in Canada. Crown corporations may be expected to play an even larger role in years ahead through joint ventures and the outright ownership of market sector firms. In the energy sector, PetroCan and CDC are increasing their holdings. The provinces have already moved in a similar direction. For example, Quebec's holding company, the Société générale de financement, has entered into a joint venture with Union Carbide and Gulf Canada to establish a world-scale petrochemical plant in Montreal called Pétromont.

Procurement

Canadian federal and provincial governments may be expected to seek ways to increase the demand for Canadian goods and services by targeting government procurement. As noted in Chapter 5, the GATT Procurement Code's coverage is limited (in Canada to a specific list of federal government entities) and does not bind the provinces' use of their own or federal monies. Thus, Canadians find themselves committed to nondiscriminatory treatment of foreign suppliers by some government entities but able to encourage buy Canadian policies by others, including some federal agencies and the provinces.

The federal government can be expected to use preferences to promote industrial development through its Procurement Review Mechanism—especially among technologically advanced industries and enterprises—to the extent possible under the code. Also, the provinces can be expected increasingly to favor domestic suppliers. As described in Chapter 6, Ontario and Quebec, as well as other provinces, have moved aggressively in this area. Further, Canadian governments can be expected to seek to persuade Crown corporations and private firms to increase Canadian sourcing: by exerting whatever influence federal and provincial governments have on the activities of

---

13 Government of Canada, *Economic Development*, p. 16.

TABLE 18. SUMMARY OF INVENTORY OF MAJOR PROJECTS TO THE YEAR 2000
   ($ Can. Millions)

SECTOR	% OF TOTAL EXPEN.	TOTAL	MULTI-PROVINCIAL OR UNDETERMINED	ATLANTIC	QUEBEC	ONTARIO	MANITOBA	SASK.	ALBERTA	B.C.	YUKON/NWT
Conventional Hydrocarbon Exploration & Development	17.8	78 150	2 500	11 500					700	250	63 200
Heavy Oil Development	9.7	42 735						1 750	40 985		
Pipelines	7.2	31 640	27 090	1 185						890	2 475
Processing & Petrochemicals	6.5	28 505		500	3 100	985		1 300	12 205	10 415	
Electrical Gen & Trans.	45.3	198 855	620	29 870	66 335	38 435	10 375	3 160	20 250	29 710	100
Forest Products	1.8	7 710		310	1 210	1 665			1 200	3 325	
Mining	4.5	19 935		1 010		4 100	500	3 965	3 230	5 625	1 505
Primary Metals Prod.	1.4	6 235		1 025	1 300	1 410	500			2 000	
Transportation	1.4	6 355		420	2 315	450			955	1 885	330
Manufacturing	3.1	13 380	8 575	400	175	4 080			150		
Defence	1.2	5 105	4 825	280							
TOTAL		438 605	43 610	46 500	74 435	51 125	11 375	10 175	79 675	54 100	67 610
% OF TOTAL EXPENDITURES			9.9	10.6	17.0	11.7	2.6	2.3	18.2	12.3	15.4

Note: Because of the wide variation of information sources, the project cost estimates included in the inventory are not stated on a consistent basis throughout. It is understood that most of the estimates are escalated to the year of expenditure by taking expected inflation rates into account. In some cases, however, other dollar bases have been utilized.

Source: Reproduced from Major Projects Task Force, *Major Canadian Projects, Major Canadian Opportunities* (Ottawa, June 1981), p. 27.

Crown corporations; by making domestic sourcing an important criteria in evaluating applications by private firms to develop natural resources on public lands; and through FIRA reviews of foreign firms planning to expand their activities in Canada.

Of particular importance to U.S. and other foreign firms supplying sophisticated, high technology capital equipment and services in Canada is that the federal government foresees considerable potential benefits from mega projects necessary to develop Canada's resources. Canada's Major Projects Task Force—a private-sector business-labor group—identified projects costing an estimated $440 billion that may be undertaken by the year 2000. The vast majority (87 percent) are in energy-related areas: electric power generation and transmission, conventional oil and gas exploration and development, heavy oil development, pipelines, hydrocarbon processing, and petrochemicals (see Table 18).[14] The task force believes the use of Canadian goods and services in these projects presents a considerable opportunity for, among other things, high quality employment; the development of Canadian indigenous technology; world-scale, internationally competitive manufacturing; and construction, engineering and service industries. To ensure that Canada obtains the maximum industrial and regional benefits, the task force made over 50 recommendations, which it summarized in the following seven points:

---

14 In the spring of 1982, doubts began emerging about the future role of mega projects in Canada's industrial development with the cancellation of the Alsands project and delays in the construction of the Alaska-Gas Pipeline. Nevertheless, to the extent that some mega projects move ahead, Ottawa may be expected to seek the maximum industrial spinoffs from their development.

- formation of a "Major Projects Assessment Agency" comprised of business and labour representatives with governments participating as observers;

- provision of continuously updated information regarding major projects since this is seen to be critical to the objective of maximizing industrial and regional benefits;

- a clear statement by governments and project participants of policies and procedures to be followed to expand Canadian ownership and participation, encourage regional equity and streamline regulatory and administrative practice;

- specific actions to improve training and utilization of manpower;

- support of good labour practices through recognition of the right of employees to organize and bargain collectively;

- high priority efforts to develop technology while limiting any disruptive effects, particularly on workers and communities;

- assistance to facilitate developments of Canadian manufacturing and service capability.[15]

Clearly, this private-sector group recommends that Canadian governments take action to maximize benefits to Canada through procurement and other forms of Canadian participation and ownership.

As discussed in Chapter 5, the government of Canada has already moved in this direction for oil and gas production on Canada Lands. As part of the National Energy Program, applicants for exploration and development permits on Canada Lands are expected to act to ensure that Canadian firms have full and equal opportunity to participate competitively in the supply of goods and services. The Committee on Megaproject Industrial and Regional Benefits will implement this policy.

The effectiveness and the impact of the C-MIRB program are not yet clear. Obviously, it responds to many of the recommendations of the Major Projects Task Force for oil and gas projects on Canada Lands, and provides guidelines of good corporate citizenship for owners and sponsors of major projects elsewhere. Extension of the C-MIRB review process to capital projects that are not on Canada Lands could prove difficult because most of these fall within the jurisdiction of provincial governments. But this does not preclude provincial initiatives, such as those taken by Alberta (see Chapter 6), and C-MIRB objectives may be applied to foreign MNCs where FIRA reviews are required.

The federal government has not yet formally responded to the recommendations of the Major Projects Task Force. But, if through cooperation with provincial governments, the C-MIRB review process (or a facsimile) is extended to all major capital projects, this would signal another major escalation of government intervention.

---

15   Major Projects Task Force, *Major Canadian Projects, Major Canadian Opportunities* (Ottawa, June 1981), pp. 10–11.

8

Conclusions: Canadian Industrial Policy and Bilateral Economic Relations

THE DIVERGENT PATHS OF U.S. AND CANADIAN POLICIES

As we have seen, over the past decade and a half the Canadian federal government has established a variety of agencies and programs to foster a pattern of industrial development consistent with its aspirations. The latter now include reduced dependence on natural resource exports through increased domestic processing and downstream manufacturing activity, greater emphasis on R&D and high technology industries, the generation of high quality employment opportunities, and a more balanced distribution of employment and income among Canada's regions.

In pursuit of these goals, Canada has traveled contrasting paths with respect to its international trade policies and its foreign investment and domestic economic policies. On the one hand, through GATT-sponsored multilateral trade negotiations, it has sought broader export opportunities and accepted more import competition. On the other hand, its policies toward new foreign investments in Canada and its approach to domestic economic development policies in general have become increasingly interventionist. The establishment of FIRA and C-MIRB, the Canadianization aspects of the NEP, and the growth of R&D and industrial incentives, public enterprises and other industrial policy tools discussed in Chapters 5 and 7 signal this trend. To some extent, these domestic policies and programs could diminish the liberalization effects of tariff reductions and other GATT-sponsored agreements to lower barriers to the flow of goods among countries.

Further, many of the provinces have evolved ambitious economic development policies that sometimes complement and sometimes conflict with Ottawa's intentions. One of the most troubling aspects of this trend is that many provincial policies are eroding the Canadian common market by creating barriers to interprovincial, as well as international, trade.

The United States has moved in a substantially different direction. While the Canadian federal government has encouraged policies to foster a pattern of industrial development consistent with a set of national goals, U.S. economic policies affecting domestic industry have concentrated more on health, safety and environmental regulation and antitrust enforcement. The emphasis has been on limiting certain adverse side effects of industrial development and neutralizing the potential for economic and environmental problems.

To be sure, the growth of U.S. regulation has been accompanied by significant programs designed to assist industries adversely affected by import competition — e.g., textiles and apparel, footwear, automobiles, shipbuilding, steel, and consumer electronics (color TVs and CB radios). Restrictions on imports through escape clause actions and orderly marketing agreements have been the principal forms of assistance. In addition, the United States has other more general programs to promote domestic industry. Examples often cited by Canadians include the tax benefits provided exporters through the Domestic International Sales Corporations (DISCs), the tax exempt status of state industrial revenue bonds, and the discriminatory procurement provisions of the Surface Transportation Assistance Act of 1979. The fact remains, however, that U.S. policies have not been fashioned to serve a consistent set of goals to guide the evolution of the U.S. economic structure, as has increasingly been the case in Canada. These divergent paths have eroded the base of experience and approach to meeting economic problems traditionally shared by the two countries.

Looking ahead, we may expect Canada to continue a far more activist and interventionist industrial policy than the United States, as its federal government attempts to balance often competing and conflicting economic and political objectives. New opportunities must be created for firms and workers in labor-intense, trade-impacted sectors or the federal government will face increasing demands to insulate them from competitive pressures with costly protectionist devices. Many other established industries that are able to regain international competitiveness must rationalize to foster greater specialization and, hence, must rely more on export markets for sales, leaving imports to provide product variety. Substantial investments, both in knowledge and physical capital, will be necessary to exploit Canada's energy resources and to ensure Canadian involvement in some of the emerging growth industries—e.g., synthetic fuels, new branches of microelectronics, biotechnology.

At the same time, political exigencies compel Canada's federal government to pursue other goals that may frustrate its ability to promote structural adjustments and the development of desirable industrial activities. These include nationalistic pressures for increased domestic control of Canadian resources and industry, and provincial pressures for a more balanced regional distribution of economic activity.

Over the next few years, the *desired* directions of change in each country promise to differ. The Canadian government's intervention in the market process may be expected to remain about the same or to increase. In contrast, the Reagan Administration is seeking to reduce the overall level of government intervention.

But neither the present Liberal government nor the Reagan Administration is finding it easy to change quickly or dramatically the overall level of government involvement in the economy. In Canada, increased intervention requires difficult political decisions about the selection of industries and regions to assist, which will undoubtedly slow the processes of policy formulation and implementation. In the United States, the unemployment and structural problems of the heavy industries concentrated in the Northeast and Midwest make total adherence to laissez-faire principles politically tough. Thus, the pace of policy change may be slower than either government might like.

As Canada moves away from what Americans view as the market paradigm and the United States seeks to rely more on the market mechanism, the similarity in the two countries' approaches to economic policy, present over much of their shared history, will erode still further. This growing contrast in the two dominant economic philosophies will inevitably make more difficult the resolution of conflicts arising out of the two countries' industrial policies.

PROSPECTIVE CONSEQUENCES OF CANADIAN POLICY FOR THE BILATERAL RELATIONSHIP

The industrial policies undertaken in both countries affect basic private-sector decisions that determine patterns of production, investment and employment: what gets produced, at what price, in what locality, owned and controlled by whom, how many people employed, and at what wage rate. But more important from a bilateral perspective, many of the policies and programs in either country affect the basic economic decisions made in the other. These spillover effects, common to industrial policies, are particularly important to the United States and Canada because of their high degree of economic interdependence.

For example, in *particular sectors and industries:*

- Canadian (U.S.) tariff and nontariff barriers to imports encourage domestic production, investment and employment but, to some extent, at the expense of comparable activities in the United States (Canada) and other countries.

- Canadian (U.S.) export incentives encourage sales in the United States (Canada) and third-country markets that displace production, investment and employment in the United States (Canada) and other countries.

- Canadian (U.S.) industrial incentives and buy national programs that promote or attract production displace imports from, or encourage exports to, the United States (Canada) and other countries, reducing production, investment and employment in them. Performance requirements imposed on foreign subsidiaries operating in Canada through FIRA reviews can have similar consequences, as can public corporations when formed to achieve industrial policy objectives.

- Canadian (U.S.) R&D incentives increase the amount of research and development taking place in North America but also attract some R&D activity at the expense of each other and third countries.

Across the *full spectrum of industry,* bilateral spillover effects may balance out somewhat. However, Canadian and U.S. policies and programs can have important consequences for the profitability of *specific firms* and the job security and employment opportunities of *selected groups of workers* on both sides of the border. Also, to the extent that Canada provides more effective incentives for industrial development than does the United States,[1] negative spillover effects may be more obvious in the United States than in Canada.[2]

In the years ahead, to the extent that Canada indeed pursues a more interventionist industrial policy and the United States relies more on the market mechanism, Canada will likely impose greater negative incremental spillover costs on the United States than vice versa. Specifically, additional Canadian measures to encourage industrial development and maintain employment—e.g., R&D and industrial incentives, discriminatory government procurement, performance requirements for foreign-controlled firms—would make exporting to Canada less profitable and/or producing in Canada for its own markets more attractive, adversely affecting U.S. competitiveness

---

1   That is, more incentives relative to the size of Canada's domestic economy.

2   With respect to third countries, the United States and Canada probably impose fewer negative spillover effects on their major trading partners than vice versa. The United States and Canada provide less direct production and export promotion subsidies than do other advanced industrial countries. See John Mutti, *Taxes, Subsidies and Competitiveness Internationally* (Washington, D.C.: Committee on Changing International Realities, 1982).

in Canadian markets. To the extent that Canada pursues its industrial policy goals through tighter controls on the activities of foreign-controlled firms, U.S. MNCs operating in Canada will be under greater pressure to undertake activities supportive of Canadian objectives, such as increasing Canadian sourcing and locating administrative activities and R&D in Canada. If these efforts are paralleled by attempts to extend Canadian ownership, U.S. MNCs could find themselves constrained from participating in a wider range of Canadian industries. (At present, foreign participation is limited in communications, natural resources, aviation, insurance, and banking.)

In the face of an activist Canadian industrial policy, adversely affected U.S. firms may seek support from the U.S. government for relief under the terms of the GATT codes governing the use of NTBs and other aspects of GATT law. However, at times existing international agreements may be inadequate both to satisfy U.S. business and labor interests and to avoid conflicts with Canada.

For example, the GATT codes governing the use of certain NTBs could serve as a useful point of departure for resolving problems resulting from many of the adverse effects of Canadian policies on U.S. interests. But, as noted earlier, the codes are limited in coverage and their potential effectiveness is not yet clear.

In this context, the Subsidy/Countervail Code is important because many of Canada's industrial policy instruments, described in Chapter 5, achieve their intended effects through direct or indirect subsidies, such as tax expenditures, preferential credits and grants and technical assistance to promote various types of industrial activity. Further, public corporations are also implicitly subsidized when they earn below-market rates of return on equity. When these programs result in subsidized exports *and material injury to U.S. industries*, the United States can countervail to protect affected firms and workers. In many instances, Canadian aid is spread thinly over many firms and industries so that the effects on U.S. industries are small and are not a serious threat. However, it is when the injury is small but noticeable that the real questions arise.

Given the high percentage of Canadian production exported to the United States, it is difficult for Canada to provide industrial subsidies without indirectly subsidizing some exports to the United States. However, since only a small share of U.S. production is exported to Canada, the converse is not true. If the United States applies a *low threshold* in defining material injury from imports before countervailing, it can ensure protection of U.S. business and labor interests but risks antagonizing the Canadian government, which views subsidies as an important and legitimate economic development tool. If the United States places a *high threshold* on material injury, it can avoid some conflicts with Canada but potentially at the expense of sacrificing some domestic business and labor interests.

Another bilateral problem could arise because the value, and consequent price effects, of many kinds of subsidies may prove difficult to measure. For example, Canadian public corporations are subsidized, potentially adversely affecting U.S. firms and workers, when they are established to maintain industrial activities that would otherwise shut down or when they are established to ensure production in locations the private sector finds uneconomic. Under these circumstances, the government is providing an implicit subsidy by accepting a below-market rate of return on its capital investment in addition to the explicit subsidy that may be required to cover operating losses. The implicit subsidy can be particularly difficult to measure.

In addition, industrial policies applied in Canada may have effects similar to subsidies but fall outside the jurisdiction of the Subsidy/Countervail Code. For example,

Quebec uses its low cost hydroelectric power to attract industries with large power requirements. Although Quebec could sell this energy to U.S. customers at higher prices, it is difficult to argue that by attracting industry with lower cost power, Quebec is offering subsidies because electricity rates vary within Canada and the United States, particularly on the basis of production costs. However, Quebec reviews applications for industrial uses of hydroelectric power in excess of 5 megawatts a year in terms of the planned activity's overall contribution to the provincial economy. To the extent that Quebec is successful in encouraging firms to locate administrative facilities and downstream production there to obtain low cost energy for operations that extensively use electricity, cheap power could then have an effect similar to a benefits-in-kind subsidy on the location of productive activities and employment in that province. However, it is not at all clear that this type of problem can be addressed under the existing Subsidy/Countervail Code (although the U.S. government could choose to invoke Section 301 of the Trade Agreements Act of 1974, discussed below).

Procurement preferences illustrate another bilateral problem emerging from Canadian industrial policy initiatives. As discussed in Chapters 5 and 7, the Canadian federal government intends to use these preferences to the extent permitted under the Procurement Code to encourage high technology industries, especially electronics. At what points do preferences for particularly promising Canadian firms displace U.S. sales in Canada? Obviously, if Canadian Firm A receives an order instead of U.S. Firm B when the latter offers a better package, discrimination is evident. Unfortunately, situations are not always clear-cut—what constitutes a better package is sometimes difficult to define—and U.S. firms and government officials could find it frustrating at times to enforce equal treatment.

Also, as discussed previously, the federal and provincial governments may require Canadian sourcing by foreign and domestic firms seeking to develop Canadian resources or by foreign firms seeking access to Canadian markets. In this regard, U.S. officials are particularly concerned about the activities of FIRA and C-MIRB. If these measures discriminate against foreign suppliers, they may be found in violation of the GATT because they deny national treatment (as required by Article III) or they tend to "nullify or impair" Canadian tariff concessions from the Tokyo Round (a violation of Article XXIII). The United States has filed a formal complaint with the GATT regarding commitments obtained from foreign firms by FIRA to purchase Canadian goods and to increase exports from Canada. A GATT panel will rule on the U.S. complaint that FIRA imposes performance requirements that accord less than equal treatment to foreign firms and distort trade. U.S. officials are monitoring the activities of the newly created C-MIRB in an effort to ensure that its reviews do not result in discrimination against U.S. firms.

In addition to the remedies that may be available under the GATT, U.S. firms could seek relief from discriminatory practices under Section 301 of the Trade Agreements Act of 1974, which permits the President to retaliate against unfair trade practices that adversely affect U.S. producers and exports. But the effects of many discriminatory policies that could potentially be the focus of Section 301 investigations are difficult to measure, and it will be hard to formulate U.S. responses to Canadian actions that are perceived both as adequate by injured American parties and fair, or at least not heavy-handed, by some Canadians.

To the extent that Canada's industrial policy programs are expanded and given sharper focus and the problems and tensions generated by bilateral spillover effects increase, the need to find suitable guidelines and means to insulate and protect U.S. (and Canadian) firms and workers from these spillovers will grow. Negotiations may be necessary just to achieve, if not to expand, the openness of trade anticipated from the Tokyo Round tariff reductions.

PROSPECTS FOR FUTURE TRADE NEGOTIATIONS

Multilateral negotiations to achieve greater control over the trade-distorting effects of national industrial policies and, possibly, to expand the tariff reductions scheduled for the 1980–87 period would be desirable. However, over the next several years, a new round of multilateral trade negotiations will not likely yield expanded codes of behavior to govern the application of industrial policies that are significantly stronger than those recently negotiated to govern nontariff barriers. In the current depressed economic environment, political pressures to pursue policies that defend domestic employment are strong. The limited coverage of the Tokyo Round codes suggests that for the time being the multilateral process may have yielded as much as possible in the form of broad agreements that are mutually acceptable to the major industrial countries.

By necessity, future negotiations to develop rules to control the trade-distorting effects of the two countries' industrial policies probably will focus on particular irritants and trade barriers and/or be conducted on a regional or bilateral basis. In this environment, several forces will encourage the United States and Canada to place more emphasis on negotiations with each other.

- The effects of many industrial policies that focus on particular sectors, such as domestic subsidies and procurement, often have their greatest impact on close neighbors or on a limited group of trading partners.

- Negotiations with industrial countries outside North America will be difficult. Those attempted with Japan with respect to its trade and industrial policies have proven to be particularly troublesome. The European Community has its own rules governing the use of many policy instruments—such as subsidies and procurements—that minimize irritants among its members but not always for its outside trading partners.[3]

Some influential Americans have expressed an interest in ways that would further open bilateral trade. The U.S. government study of the desirability of U.S. entry into trade agreements with countries in the northern portion of the Western Hemisphere mandated by Section 1104 of the Trade Agreements Act of 1979 signals at least some interest within the legislative branch of the U.S. government. Further, President Reagan, while still a candidate in 1979, spoke out on the potential benefits of a North American accord, which would strengthen economic ties with both Canada and Mexico.

---

3   The EC Commission has the authority to review various forms of subsidies and incentives and rule on the complaints of firms on the practices of other countries. Using this power, it has limited Italian aid to textile manufacturers, probably benefiting countries inside and outside the Community. However, in a case dealing with the British Export Development Corporation, the resolution of the dispute only dealt with the terms provided for British exports to other EC countries and did not address the terms provided other customers. Further, aid to high technology industries that compete most directly with those of the United States, but not with those of other EC nations, has faced few limitations.

No Canadian government since 1948 has been interested in negotiating a comprehensive free trade agreement with the United States, and the present Liberal government is not likely to do so. Instead, since regaining power in March 1980, it has announced new industrial policy initiatives whose combined effects could well adversely influence the present degree of openness of the bilateral flow of goods and capital. And, as discussed in Chapter 7, any agreement to liberalize trade further across a wide range of industries could conflict with such policies because it would have to incorporate provisions to reduce nontariff barriers. Nevertheless, some groups outside the government have expressed interest in a trade agreement with the United States.[4] Also, some Canadians are interested in negotiations that focus on particular barriers or sectors but, as noted in Chapter 7, achieving such agreements presents special problems.

It hardly need be stated that Canada, like all U.S. trading partners, would approach any bilateral negotiation pragmatically, seeking to balance opportunities for additional exports against transition costs. However, Canada would likely want more than balance-of-employment gains and losses and a suitable ratio of consumer benefits to adjustment costs. Regardless of whether negotiations focused on particular trade barriers or particular sectors, Canada could be expected to place high priority on seeking opportunities consistent with its industrial policy goals and, to some degree or other, it would likely be willing to sacrifice some of the efficiency gains that may be achieved in fashioning trade liberalization agreements to achieve these objectives. And Canada would seek performance commitments and safeguards to ensure that the desired benefits and opportunities do, in fact, materialize.

The time is not propitious to consider U.S. negotiations with Canada to establish a comprehensive free trade arrangement because the Canadian government is currently pursuing activist, and in some cases nationalistic, industrial policies in an effort to cope with substantial structural economic problems. For now, the United States may find it productive to explore with Canada ways to improve—perhaps to some extent replace—existing processes and mechanisms so that the two countries can deal more effectively with current bilateral economic disputes and head off emerging and potential ones. Specifically, the new arrangements could provide:

- objective fact-finding and neutral analyses and assessments of present and prospective policy initiatives in one country—including those emanating from provinces and states—that are causing, or might cause, ill effects in the other;
- a forum to discuss the effects of such policy initiatives; and
- mediation facilities when both countries agree to seek such services.[5]

Such processes and mechanisms could be a forerunner of stronger institutions for implementing future bilateral agreements designed to limit the trade-distorting effects of the two countries' domestic economic policies.

---

4   The Economic Council of Canada endorsed multicountry free trade agreements as the optimal course for Canada and a bilateral agreement with the United States as the next best option in Economic Council of Canada, *Looking Outward: A New Trade Strategy for Canada* (Ottawa, 1975). The Canadian Senate also expressed strong interest in a bilateral agreement in Canadian Senate, Standing Committee on Foreign Affairs, *Canada-United States Relations: Canada's Trade Relations with the United States,* Vols. II and III (Ottawa: Queen's Printer, 1978 and 1982).

5   A specific proposal along these lines was issued by the Canadian-American Committee in October 1981 in *Improving Bilateral Consultation on Economic Issues* (Washington: NPA, 1981). A somewhat similar recommendation is offered in "Canada, the United States and the World Economy," by Marie-Losec Drouin and Harald B. Malmgren, *Foreign Affairs,* Winter 1981/82.

The Development of Canadian Policy
Regarding Automotive Trade with the United States

The Automotive Agreement (negotiated in 1964 and enacted in 1965) is justly seen to be the most important event of the 1960s in terms of its effects on bilateral trade. It deserves also to be regarded as a major step in the evolution of Canada's implicit industrial policy. For the unilateral Canadian initiatives of the early 1960s that precipitated negotiations on auto trade with the United States and the performance requirements imposed on U.S. firms—both within the resulting bilateral treaty and by undertakings to Canada acting unilaterally—revealed that country's new willingness to:

- manipulate trade policy to achieve industrial policy objectives;

- strike bargains with foreign-owned firms by offering conditions benefiting their operations in Canada in exchange for commitments to perform in *specified ways* that furthered Canada's goals for its industry.

By 1960, Canadians had become concerned over the decreasing ability of domestic automotive production to hold its previously dominant position in supplying the Canadian market. New vehicles production had slipped from 110 percent of apparent consumption in 1952 to only somewhat over 70 percent by 1959 and 1960 (see Table A-1). This decline occurred despite a "content requirement," which since 1936 had encouraged vehicle production in Canada by permitting a firm so engaged to import certain components duty free if 60 percent of the factory cost of the vehicle was supplied domestically.

BLADEN'S EXTENDED CONTENT PLAN (1961)

A Royal Commission of one, Vincent Bladen, was appointed in 1960 to recommend measures to increase production of Canadian vehicles and exports.[1] Bladen's report, issued in August 1961, recommended seven measures.[2] The most important of these would extend the application of Canada's 1936 content requirements. Specifically, Bladen would widen the scope of automotive production in Canada eligible to earn duty remission on imports from merely what was incorporated within vehicles assembled there to include Canadian-made components that were exported for assembly elsewhere. Given the considerable value to auto makers in Canada of relief from then high duties on automotive imports, the extended content plan would have offered significant incentive for Canadian production of auto parts for export.

---

1 Bladen also hoped that his proposals would reconcile industrial and consumer interests, often a difficult tradeoff in industrial strategy. His concluding paragraph opens with this interesting statement: "The problem, as I came to see it during the progress of my inquiry, was how to reconcile the desire of the consumer for low prices and of the industry for increased protection. I believe that the solution lies in an effective method of protection which is expansionist rather than restrictive. This solution may be said to maintain protection but reduce the burden of protection. . . ." *Report of Royal Commission on the Automotive Industry* (Bladen Report), (Ottawa: Queens Printer, 1961), pp. 77–78.

2 Ibid., pp. 57ff. Only one of these is discussed here. The other six were intended to relieve the tax burden on the industry and to improve its competitive position.

TABLE A-1. BASIC INDICATORS OF THE CANADIAN AUTOMOTIVE INDUSTRY,
1952, 1955, 1959, AND 1960
(Thousands of Motor Vehicles)

	1952	1955	1959	1960
(1) Production in Canada	434	454	368	396
(2) Exports	80	35	19	23
(3) Imports	39	58	166	180
(4) Net trade (2 minus 3)	+41	−23	−147	−157
(5) Apparent consumption (1 minus 4)	393	477	515	553
(6) Domestic production as a percent of apparent consumption	110%	95%	71%	72%

Source: Lines 1, 2, and 3, *Report of Royal Commission on the Automotive Industry* (Bladen Report), (Ottawa: Queens Printer, 1961), pp. 14–15 (1960 data preliminary).

THE DUTY REMISSION PLANS, 1962 AND 1963

A variation of Bladen's proposal, the first of two so-called duty remission plans, was applied in November 1962 to stimulate Canadian automotive parts exports. The 25 percent duty paid by a Canadian automobile producer on imported automatic transmissions and stripped engines (up to 10,000 engines for each producer) was remitted to the extent that the Canadian content of automotive parts now exported exceeded that of the 12-month base period just ended.

One year later this pilot plan was generalized. Duties were remitted on all imports of motor vehicles and original equipment parts to the extent that the company in question increased the Canadian content of its exports of all automotive products above that of the base period.

Table A-2 notes these two variations of the duty remission plan and the subsequent sevenfold increase in Canadian automotive exports to the United States between 1962 and 1964. Of this development, the U.S. Tariff Commission concluded in 1965:

> Although other factors, such as the strong demand for automobiles in the U.S. market, were important influences, the increases in exports were large enough to suggest that the duty rebate plan played a significant role.[3]

In any event, specific impacts of Canada's actions on automotive production in the United States were soon evident. One was the transfer of Studebaker's vehicle assembly from Indiana to Ontario. "Referring to the expanded plan, a spokesman for the company stated that the 'economic climate in Canada thus established and, of course, the timing, were tailor-made for our move to Canada.' "[4]

Of greater consequence, however, were the effects that the Canadian performance incentives were seen to have on bilateral trade of auto parts. The benefits to be gained by U.S. firms from remission of Canadian duties would encourage them to source components for U.S. vehicle assembly from Canada rather than from traditional and slightly lower cost U.S. suppliers. In the test case, an independent U.S. radiator firm, considering itself victimized by this situation, triggered a U.S. Treasury investigation into whether the duty remission scheme was in effect an export subsidy as defined under U.S. law. Sensitivity of the U.S. Administration to the probable

---

3   From Report of the U.S. Tariff Commission to the House Ways and Means Committee on the Automotive Products Trade Act of 1965 (April 23, 1965), as reprinted in the *Hearings on the Agreement before the Senate Finance Committee*, 89th Cong., 1st sess., H. Rept. 9042 (1965), p. 385.

4   Ibid.

TABLE A-2. UNILATERAL CANADIAN AUTOMOTIVE TARIFF POLICIES BEFORE THE AUTOMOTIVE AGREEMENT, AND EXPORTS TO THE UNITED STATES

		Canadian Automotive Exports to U.S. ($U.S. millions)		
Year	Canadian Policy Developments	Automotive Parts	Complete Vehicles	Total
1961	No new policy (content requirements of 1936 in effect).	8.7	2.1	10.8
1962	From November, unilateral Canadian duty remission applied to imported engines and transmissions.	9.5	2.6	12.1
1963	From November, unilateral Canadian duty remission extended to *all* imported vehicles and original equipment parts.	30.3	3.5	33.8
1964	Extended duty remissions in effect. Bilateral negotiations leading to the Automotive Agreement began in April after U.S. Treasury investigation of the 1963 scheme began. (Canada removed all unilateral tariff rebate schemes on January 15, 1965 upon inauguration of the Automotive Agreement.)	65.3	24.1	89.4

Source: Report of U.S. Tariff Commission to the House Ways and Means Committee, *The Automotive Products Trade Act of 1965,* Table 5, 89th Cong., H. Rept. 6960, as reprinted in the *Hearings on the Agreement before the Senate Finance Committee,* 89th Cong., 1st sess., H. Rept. 9042 (1965), p. 448.

consequences of having to impose countervailing duties on Canada at that time contributed to a receptive attitude toward the bold plan that emerged as the Automotive Agreement.

THE AUTOMOTIVE AGREEMENT (1965)

Subject to certain conditions, the agreement established duty free trade between the two countries in new vehicles and original equipment parts. The agreement is noteworthy on two points.

(1) It does not provide free trade in the usual sense, but rather uses duty free imports to gain performance commitments from foreign MNCs;

(2) this kind of bargain made it a milestone in Canada's evolving policy toward foreign investment.

On the first point, what sold the agreement to the U.S. firms producing vehicles in Canada — the elimination of high Canadian tariffs on new vehicles and components for them — was strictly conditional on their meeting two sets of performance requirements.

• The agreement itself obliged each producer in Canada (a) to continue the growth of *vehicle assembly* there and (b) to maintain the Canadian content at no less than the absolute dollar value achieved in the 1964 model year.

• Supplementary "letters of undertaking" by the four major U.S. car manufacturers committed them *to increase their value added* in Canada by specified amounts.

Thus, the agreement extends the kinds of incentives implemented in 1962 and 1963 but with the important difference that its array of commitments was partially encompassed in a bilateral treaty rather than in unilateral Canadian action. However, the supplementary commitments by the four U.S. firms echoed the previous unilateral approach insomuch as Canada was the sole governmental party to the agreement.

On the second point, the swap of benefits agreed to between the Canadian government and the U.S. auto firms is a precursor of the far more generalized bargain whereby FIRA requires foreign-owned firms across the board to meet performance targets in return for permission to expand their Canadian operations.

Another aspect of the automotive agreement is, however, quite incompatible with contemporary Canadian aspirations for industrial policy. The various commitments, now frozen into the agreement, permitted—indeed encouraged—the U.S. firms to meet their performance goals in Canada by assembling vehicles rather than by manufacturing components, an activity requiring the higher levels of skills and technology that Canadian policy now seeks to encourage. (Ironically, Bladen's proposal and the first duty remission scheme clearly favored Canadian parts production.) The subsequent distribution of production between the two countries, at least as revealed in bilateral trade statistics,[5] shows an emphasis on parts production in the United States and vehicle assembly in Canada.

---

5   Bilateral trade statistics, which are relentlessly cited by Canadians as showing this division of production, automatically introduce massive distortions by not recognizing that the majority of U.S.-made parts shipped to Canada return to the U.S. market in Canadian-assembled cars. An exercise at NPA in 1978 to eliminate repatriated parts from bilateral trade statistics revealed a Canadian surplus of parts exports that did not return, and a U.S. surplus of vehicles.

Appendix 2

Evolution of Canadian Regional Policy

Per capita incomes and economic welfare vary substantially among and within Canada's provinces. The federal government has long been committed to programs that seek to compensate for and reduce these imbalances. Therefore, regional aid is directed to designated areas throughout Canada.

The evolution of Canada's approach to regional policy goes back to 1957 with the establishment of fiscal equalization payments. The program transfers revenues from the federal government to lower income provinces to ensure that adequate levels of public services are available through the country. During 1981–82, the grants were about $4.0 billion or about 6 percent of the federal budget and are expected to maintain roughly that share over the next several years:[1]

	1979–80	1980–81	1981–82	1982–83	1983–84	1984–85
Equalization payments ($ billions)	3.3	3.5	4.0	4.6	5.2	5.8
Percent of federal budget	6.2	6.0	5.8	6.0	6.1	6.2

During the 1960s, there was a growing consensus that income transfers were insufficient because they did not adequately address the causes of lagging economic development and personal incomes in economically depressed areas. As a consequence, several programs and agencies were established to improve development prospects in these regions. Among these were the Agricultural and Rural Development Act programs (1961) and the Fund for Rural Economic Development (1966). The latter sought to attack rural poverty through federal/provincial agreements with New Brunswick, Prince Edward Island, Quebec, and Manitoba. Also, the Atlantic Development Board (1962) was established to assist in infrastructure development in that region. Finally the Area Development Act (1963) provided incentives to manufacturing firms to locate facilities in depressed areas.

By 1969, it was apparent that these agencies did not offer a consistent approach to regional policy, and they were consolidated under the new Department of Regional Economic Expansion. DREE was conceived to provide more balance and coordination in the government's approach to regional problems. The department's objectives were:

> . . . to facilitate social adjustments in Canada through federal-provincial agreements, special programs and other activities designed to increase, and improve access to, development opportunities in various regions of the country.[2]

---

1   Department of Finance, *The Budget* (Ottawa, October 28, 1980); *The Budget in More Detail* (Ottawa, November 12, 1981); *Fiscal Arrangements in the Eighties—Proposals of the Government of Canada* (Ottawa, November 1981). In fiscal years 1977–78 through 1980–81, the four Atlantic provinces, Quebec, Manitoba, and Saskatchewan received payments. In 1981–82, Saskatchewan did not qualify for payment and is not expected to qualify over the next several years under the payments formula proposed by Ottawa in November 1981.

2   Statistics Canada, *Canada Yearbook 1978–79* (Ottawa, 1979), p. 894.

DREE was reorganized in 1973 in an effort to decentralize the administration of its programs and make them more responsive to local needs. Programs were administered through its headquarters in Ottawa, regional offices in Moncton, Montreal, Toronto, and Saskatoon, and various provincial branch offices. Its activities could be divided into three broad areas: General Development Agreements (GDAs), Regional Development Incentives Program (RDIP), and rural development programs.

DREE entered into GDAs with the provinces, which provided 10-year frameworks for coordinated regional development activities. These agreements covered infrastructure development, specific sectors' needs—such as in agriculture, tourism, minerals—and special problem areas—such as northland development. The plans outlined in GDAs were implemented through Special Development Agreements in which the federal government provided 50 to 90 percent of the funds.

Under the authority of RDIA, DREE also provided grants, direct loans and loan guarantees that encouraged the establishment of enterprises in designated development areas. Most manufacturing and processing industries were eligible. Notable exclusions were pulp and paper and mining.

DREE administered several rural development programs. Its total 1979–80 expenditures were $590 million, and of this, $360 million was spent through GDAs and $109 million was spent on direct industrial incentives (e.g., through RDIA).

In January 1982, DREE was dissolved as part of a larger government reorganization designed to give greater emphasis to regional development problems and exports in formulating economic policy. The Canadian government announced that the Ministry of State for Economic Development would be renamed the Ministry of State for Economic and Regional Development (MSERD) and would be responsible for providing the Cabinet Committee on Economic and Regional Development (CCERD) with analysis and information on regional development issues. The objective is to ensure that regional development concerns are given adequate consideration in the formulation of the full range of national economic policies.

It was announced that the MSERD would establish regional offices in each province headed by a federal Economic Development Coordinating Committee to serve four functions:

- to provide an improved regional information base for decisionmaking by the Cabinet Committee on Economic and Regional Development, for use particularly in the development of regionally sensitive economic development strategies;

- to give regional officials of government departments a better understanding of the decisions and objectives of the Cabinet;

- to better coordinate the implementation of government decisions affecting economic development in the regions;

- and to frame regional economic development policies for consideration by the Cabinet.

The responsibilities for administering existing DREE programs—e.g., GDAs, RDIA incentives— were transferred to the new Department of Regional Industrial Expansion.

In January 1982, the Canadian government also announced that the CCERD, with the assistance of the MSERD, will review the regional implications of all major economic development programs. Further, it was announced that while existing GDAs will remain in place until their expiration dates, these agreements will be replaced by new and simpler agreements covering a wider range of federal departments and programs. These agreements will be developed by the MSERD.

It is too early to assess the implications of the January 1982 reorganization of regional policymaking and implementation responsibilities. However, three observations about the state of Canada's regional policy prior to the reorganization are relevant.

First, taken together, federal equalization payments and DREE expenditures totaled only about $3.9 billion or 7.4 percent of the federal budget in 1979–80. Of this total, DREE expenditures were about 15.1 percent and direct industrial incentives were only about 3.3 percent. Thus, federal regional aid has been mostly directed toward transfers and infrastructure development.

Second, the resources devoted to directly encouraging private investment in depressed regions are focused on the manufacturing and processing sectors. As such, Canadian regional industrial incentives are designed to support the overriding industrial policy goal of developing the manufacturing and processing sectors. However, these resources are quite small, and it is not at all clear how effective they have been in inducing additional investment. Critics often claimed that more than a significant portion of DREE's investment incentives have gone to enterprises that would have located in the same depressed areas without such assistance. Of course, the creation of such windfalls was not DREE's intention, and the validity of this criticism is difficult to establish clearly or dispose of empirically.

Third, while the federal equalization payments and the activities of DREE have composed the most important parts of Canada's regional aid program, many other federal programs also redistribute income to the provinces. An indirect "evening" influence arises from uneven levels of per capita taxable income among the provinces. In addition, there are a variety of other programs funded—especially shared-cost programs in fields such as education and health care—involving substantial federal transfers to provincial governments. In fiscal year 1979–80, transfers to provincial governments amounted to about $11.2 billion or about 15.8 percent of the federal budget. Equalization payments and transfers for economic development assistance were only about 29 percent of total transfers. Table A-3 shows a breakdown of these transfers and indicates that the federal government provides substantial transfers for a variety of social services and, in addition, tax transfers of about $3.9 billion.[3]

---

3   The data in Table A-3 and cited in this paragraph are estimates for 1979–80 compiled somewhat earlier than the data cited elsewhere in this appendix, which come from expenditure documents compiled after the end of the fiscal year and do not coincide exactly with the estimates in Table A-3.

TABLE A-3. FEDERAL TRANSFERS TO THE PROVINCES, TERRITORIES AND MUNICIPALITIES, FISCAL YEAR 1979-80 ESTIMATES
($ Can. Millions)

Program	Nfld.	P.E.I.	N.S.	N.B.	Que.	Ont.	Man.	Sask.	Alta.	B.C.	N.W.T.	Yukon	Total
Equalization	340.0	77.1	405.3	336.2	1,362.3	—	233.5	39.1	—	—	—	—	2,793.5
Statutory Subsidies	9.7	.7	2.2	1.8	4.5	5.5	2.2	2.1	3.3	2.1	—	—	34.1
1971 Undistributed Income on Hand	.1	*	.3	.2	5.6	5.7	.7	.4	1.6	1.9	—	—	16.5
Public Utilities Income Tax Transfer	4.0	.6	—	—	1.3	7.6	.4	*	29.7	.6	.1	.2	44.5
Youth Allowances Recovery	—	—	—	—	-141.2	—	—	—	—	—	—	—	-141.2
Reciprocal Taxation	5.3	3.2	15.4	8.2	33.2	45.0	—	—	—	—	—	—	110.3
Prior Years Adjustments**													50.0
Total Fiscal Transfer Cash Payments	359.1	81.6	423.2	346.4	1,265.7	63.8	236.8	41.6	34.6	4.6	.1	.2	2,907.7
Hospital Insurance	66.9	14.4	98.9	81.9	529.9	928.7	120.7	111.9	207.5	271.8	4.9	2.0	2,439.5
Medicare	23.1	5.0	34.0	28.2	182.6	320.0	41.5	38.5	71.5	93.7	1.7	.7	840.5
Post-Secondary Education	42.2	9.1	62.3	51.6	333.8	585.0	76.0	70.4	130.7	171.2	3.1	1.3	1,536.7
Extended Health Care	14.2	3.0	20.9	17.3	155.1	210.0	25.5	23.5	49.4	63.3	1.1	.5	583.8
Prior Year Adjustments**													74.5
Established Programs Financing Cash Payment	146.4	31.5	216.1	179.0	1,201.4	2,043.7	263.7	244.3	459.1	600.0	10.8	4.5	5,475.0
Canada Assistance Plan	44.4	9.4	58.2	74.4	508.4	468.4	62.9	61.8	145.3	230.8	7.9	1.4	1,673.3
Health Resources Fund	—	.5	2.0	—	.6	.8	.5	—	.4	2.7	—	—	7.5
Other Health and Welfare	1.1	.3	2.7	2.0	6.0	43.6	5.3	3.7	7.2	1.1	.1	.6	73.7
Official Languages	1.9	1.1	3.5	15.4	99.5	41.8	5.3	2.0	4.9	4.9	.1	.2	180.6
Economic Development	56.7	29.3	39.8	52.9	139.4	24.8	24.0	19.4	8.1	19.5	2.0	1.5	417.4
Crop Insurance	*	.6	.1	.1	2.9	8.6	8.0	32.3	16.0	1.4	—	—	70.0
Territorial Financial Agreements											202.7	51.2	253.9
Municipal Grants	1.2	.6	8.0	4.4	34.9	61.5	8.0	3.5	9.0	14.9	1.3	.7	148.0
Total Other Cash Payments	105.3	41.8	114.3	149.2	791.7	649.5	114.0	122.7	190.9	275.3	214.1	55.6	2,824.4
TOTAL CASH TRANSFERS	610.8	154.9	753.6	674.6	3,258.8	2,757.0	614.5	408.6	684.6	879.9	225.0	60.3	11,207.1
Established Programs Financing Tax Transfer													
13.5 Personal Income Tax Points	39.7	7.9	71.9	54.7	720.7	1,180.5	105.2	94.1	279.7	372.4	5.6	3.9	2,936.3
1.0 Corporate Income Tax Point	2.0	.4	3.7	3.1	48.7	91.4	9.0	9.0	45.8	27.1	.6	.2	241.0
Contracting-Out Tax Transfer													
8.5 Personal Income Tax Points for EPF	—	—	—	—	412.3	—	—	—	—	—	—	—	412.3
5.0 Personal Income Tax Points for CAP	—	—	—	—	217.4	—	—	—	—	—	—	—	217.4
3.0 Personal Income Tax Points for Youth Allowances	—	—	—	—	141.2	—	—	—	—	—	—	—	141.2
TOTAL TAX TRANSFERS	41.7	8.3	75.6	57.8	1,540.3	1,271.9	114.2	103.1	325.5	399.5	6.2	4.1	3,948.2
TOTAL CASH PLUS TRANSFERS	652.5	163.2	829.2	732.4	4,799.1	4,028.9	728.7	511.7	1,010.1	1,279.4	231.2	64.4	15,155.3
Equalization — Dollars per capita	592	627	479	479	216	—	226	41	—	—	—	—	—

*Amount too small to be expressed.
**Distribution not available by province and territory.

Source: Atlantic Provinces Economic Council, *The Atlantic Vision-1990* (Halifax, 1979), Table 4-5, pp. 66-67. Reproduced with permission.